GREATEST GAMES
OF THE
STANLEY CUP
The Battles and the Rivalries

J. Alexander Poulton

OVER
TIME
BOOKS

The Publisher: Overtime Books is an imprint of Éditions de
    la Montagne Verte

Library and Archives Canada Cataloguing in Publication

Poulton, J. Alexander (Jay Alexander), 1977–
    Greatest games of the Stanley Cup : the battles and the rivalries /
    J. Alexander Poulton.

Includes bibliographical references.
ISBN-13: 978-1-897277-06-5
ISBN-10: 1-897277-06-7

    1. Stanley Cup (Hockey)—History. 2. National Hockey
League—History. I. Title.

GV847.7.P69 2006   796.962'648   C2006-901822-7

Project Director: J. Alexander Poulton
Project Editor: Nicholle Carrière
Cover Image: Courtesy of *The Edmonton Journal*, photo by Brian Gavriloff. (1988 Edmonton Oilers Stanley Cup Champions: Esa Tikkanen, Steve Smith, Mark Messier, Wayne Gretzky and Kevin Lowe.)

PC:P5

Dedication

To Nana, for all her love and support

Contents

PART II: THE NEW LEAGUE

Introduction

The Stanley Cup has always held a special place in the hearts and dreams of everyone who watches and plays the game of hockey. Since the Cup was first awarded in 1893, it has been the ultimate goal of every team to win the trophy. In the Cup's first two decades of existence, the lengths some teams went to win Lord Stanley's silverware established a mystique around the Cup that only grew over the years and made it an even more desirable goal for all professional hockey players as the ultimate achievement of their careers.

The story of the Dawson City Nuggets in 1905 perfectly illustrates the single-mindedness of a team to win hockey's ultimate prize. Before the Stanley Cup became the exclusive property of the National Hockey League, it was awarded to the best team in all of Canada, and the previous winner could be challenged by any team approved by the Cup's trustees. In 1905, the Ottawa Silver Seven were the reigning Stanley Cup champions, and the Dawson City Nuggets wanted to take that title away from the upper-class team from the nation's capital. The Nuggets faced two very significant obstacles in their quest to win the Stanley Cup. First, the Silver Seven, led by Frank "One Eye" McGee, had the best players at their disposal, and secondly, the Dawson City team was more than 4000 miles away from the site of the final game in Ottawa. But the opportunity to win the Cup was too good to pass up despite the obvious challenges. The Nuggets set out on the journey from the Yukon by bicycle, boat, train and foot, finally arriving at their destination 23 days later. The two teams would play a two-game series in which the winner would be the team that scored the most goals in the two games. Unfortunately, the Nuggets were no match for the highly skilled Silver Seven, who beat them in the two-game series by a combined score of 32–4, with Frank McGee scoring a record 14 goals in the second game alone. No matter, however. By then the Nuggets were a hit with the public, who had gotten wind of their epic adventure, and the team would always be remembered for their sheer nerve and desire to win the Stanley Cup.

But as hockey became more popular and teams began sprouting up all over Canada and the United States, new professional leagues were formed, and the Cup went to the select few teams who could afford the best players. In the beginning, it was the Ottawa Silver Seven (later renamed the Ottawa Senators) who had the best players, such as Fred "Cyclone" Taylor, Percy LeSueur, Cy Denney and Frank Nighbor, but soon other teams found superstars of their own, such as the Montréal Wanderers' Lester Patrick and defensive specialist Si Griffis. Hockey owes a great deal to these early pioneers, for without their dedication and passion for the game during a time when there were few rewards other than playing for the love of the sport (and of course, the Stanley Cup), hockey would not be around today.

New teams began their first years of operation in leagues that started up all over North America. From amateur leagues such as the Amateur Hockey Association of Canada, established in 1899, to the early pro league of the National Hockey Association (NHA), established in 1909, hockey was here to stay. Many teams would fold, but a few would last through financial difficulties and make history of their own. The Montréal Canadiens organization was formed in late 1909 and joined the fledgling NHA for the start of their season in 1910, and the Toronto Maple Leafs (originally known as the Toronto Arenas) began their first year of operation when the NHA folded and became the National Hockey League in 1917.

In the National Hockey League's first season, the Toronto Arenas won the Stanley Cup by beating the Pacific Coast Hockey Association (PCHA) champions, the Vancouver Millionaires. With the league's future already in question, the NHL started the 1918–19 season with just three teams scheduled to play only 18 regular season games. The Montréal Canadiens came out as the champions of the NHL finals and traveled west to take on the Seattle Metropolitans of the PCHA, but the series was eventually canceled because of the global influenza epidemic (Canadiens defenseman Joe Hall eventually died from the disease), and no Stanley Cup champion was named for the first time since the trophy was awarded in 1893. (Of course, it wouldn't be the last time this happened.)

Over the next few years, the National Hockey League would see its first dynasty, with the Ottawa Senators winning the Cup three times in four years. The NHL added the first American team in 1924, and in 1926, the Cup would become sole property of the National Hockey

League. In the first few years of the National Hockey League playoffs, players such as Howie Morenz, Cy Denney, Aurel Joliat, Georges Vezina, Punch Broadbent, Nels Stewart, Newsy Lalonde and Clint Benedict would all have their names engraved on the trophy, winning some of the most memorable finals in NHL history.

As the decades passed, new teams and new players made places for themselves in the history books with their playoff heroics. Howie Morenz electrified Montréal Canadiens fans (and fans pretty much everywhere he went) with his amazing speed and natural scoring ability on the ice. He led the Canadiens to three Stanley Cup championships before passing away tragically in 1937. Eddie Shore, legendary defenseman for the Boston Bruins, led his team to their first Cup win in 1929 and again 10 years later in 1939, this time with the help of rookie goaltending sensation Frank Brimsek. The Detroit Red Wings would win their first of 10 Stanley Cups in 1936 with famous players such as Syd Howe, Hec Kilrea and Mud Bruneteau (who scored the goal that ended the longest overtime game in playoff history against the Montréal Maroons in the sixth overtime period). The 1940s would herald some major changes in the NHL, most notably the "Age of the Dynasty," when the league was whittled down to just six teams.

With only a handful of teams in the league, there was a significant pool of talent for the teams to choose from, and when a player joined an organization, he often stayed with them for his entire career, giving successful teams long periods in which they dominated the league. The first such "dynasty" was the Toronto Maple Leafs of the late 1940s, led by players such as Ted Kennedy, Syl Apps and goaltender Turk Broda, who won the Cup three times in a row from 1947 to 1949. Although the Red Wings of the early 1950s dominated the regular season with players such as Terry Sawchuk, Gordie Howe and Ted Lindsay, they failed to put together a string of Stanley Cup victories that would have made them a dynasty. Then the Montréal Canadiens came along in the late 1950s and defined what a dynasty truly is and what every team aspired to be. Stacked with Hall of Fame players such as Maurice "Rocket" Richard, Jean Beliveau, Jacques Plante, Dickie Moore, Bernie Geoffrion, Doug Harvey and Henri Richard, the Canadiens would win five consecutive championships and make their mark in Stanley Cup history.

Chicago would win the Cup in 1961, but it was the Toronto Maple Leafs and the Montréal Canadiens who would trade the Stanley Cup back and forth over the next decade, until the Boston Bruins and a young defenseman named

Bobby Orr broke the trend in 1970. Over the next few years, the league would undergo several expansions and new teams would get the chance to win the league's ultimate prize. The Philadelphia Flyers, New York Islanders, Edmonton Oilers, Calgary Flames and Pittsburgh Penguins would all make their mark in the playoffs and take home the Cup as champions.

But through all the years and all the changes in hockey, the goal has remained the same. The first time a young player puts on his skates and dreams of making it to the National Hockey League, he has one purpose in mind—to hold the Stanley Cup high above his head. It has become more than just a trophy—it has come to symbolize the passion and pain with which every player has fought to earn the right and privilege to be called a Stanley Cup champion. One just has to look at the picture of Bobby Hull flying through the air after scoring the Stanley Cup–winning goal in the 1970 finals to understand the sheer glory that comes with winning the sport's ultimate prize.

Part I
THE EARLY YEARS

Chapter One

The First Stanley Cup Victory

By the 1880s, hockey was exploding in popularity across Canada. From frozen ponds to well-maintained skating rinks, hockey was quickly becoming the favorite pastime of Canadians, whether they were watching the game or playing it. Americans were slower to jump on the hockey bandwagon, but as time went on, a few organizations began popping up in the northern cities. By the early 1900s, several teams were operating in both amateur and professional leagues. When Sir Frederick Arthur Stanley, Baron Stanley of Preston, arrived in Canada in 1888 to assume his duties as Governor General, he was quick to note the popularity of the game that was sweeping the nation and decided to create a trophy that would be awarded annually to the best team in the country. Lord Stanley wrote of his intentions in a letter to an aide after he had returned to England:

"There does not appear to be any outward sign of the championship at present. Considering the interest that hockey matches now elicit and the importance of having the games fairly played under generally recognized rules, I am willing to give a cup that should be annually held by the winning club."

Lord Stanley had a trophy made by a London silversmith for about $50, and it was shipped off to Canada, where two trustees were given the responsibility of picking the teams that would fight for the right to hold the Cup. At the end of the 1893 season, the Cup was awarded to the winners of the Amateur Hockey Association (AHA) championship, the Montréal Amateur Athletic Association, without any other teams competing for the Cup in a playoff round. The first actual competition for the Cup took place one year later in 1894, when at the end of the AHA regular season, three teams vied for possession of Lord Stanley's Cup. The first-ever Stanley Cup playoff game was held on St. Patrick's Day between the Montréal Victorias and the Montréal AAA. The AAAs won the game by a score of 3–2 and then went on the following year to defeat the Ottawa Capitals, winning the Stanley Cup for the second year in a row.

As the popularity of hockey and the prestige of winning Lord Stanley's Cup grew with each passing year, more and more teams vied for the honor of being the champion of the country's newest and most popular sport. With this newfound interest in the game, certain players began to shine above others, and teams negotiated heavily with the best players in order to secure themselves the best chance of winning the Cup. Hockey fever was born, and it was here to stay.

Chapter Two

The Silver Seven Dynasty

As the popularity and glory of the Stanley Cup grew, one team emerged as the dominant force in hockey, able to challenge almost every year for possession of hockey's ultimate prize. The Ottawa Silver Seven, later known as the Ottawa Senators, was the premier team in hockey before the establishment of the National Hockey League and also for the first decade of the new league. From 1903 to 1923, Ottawa won eight Stanley Cup titles, and some of the best players ever to put on a pair of skates had passed through their ranks. Alf Smith, Harvey Pulford, Fred "Cyclone" Taylor, Clint Benedict, Harry "Punch" Broadbent and, most famous and the greatest of all, Frank "One Eye" McGee, are just a few of the Ottawa players whose names are engraved on Lord Stanley's Cup, testifying to the skill that the team had at its disposal in those years.

McGee was at the center of Ottawa's initial Stanley Cup championship in 1903, using his considerable speed and remarkable stickhandling ability to secure his place in hockey history as one of the best natural goal-scorers to ever touch a puck. McGee's accomplishments were even more remarkable considering that he could only see out of one eye owing to an injury that occurred while playing hockey. Also, at the time there were seven players on the ice, and no forward passing was allowed. McGee's most famous moment came in 1905, when a ragtag team of players from Dawson City challenged the Silver Seven for the right to be named Stanley Cup champions. The Silver Seven easily defeated the Dawson City Nuggets 9–2 in the first match, but it was in the second match that Ottawa really embarrassed their opponents. In the most lopsided Stanley Cup game ever, the Ottawa Silver Seven scored 23 goals to the Nuggets' 2 before the final whistle blew, ending the massacre. McGee, for his part, solidified his place in hockey folklore by scoring the most points in a professional game, netting 14 goals, three of which he scored within 90 seconds and another four in 140 seconds.

Ottawa had established itself as the premier club in Canada. They played a fast and rough game that drew several thousand fans every time the team stepped onto the ice. But after their third Stanley Cup victory in a row, things started to go downhill for the boys from the nation's capital when they met the Montréal Wanderers for the 1906 Stanley Cup challenge. The two-game series was a close one, but the Wanderers came out on top, outscoring the Silver Seven 12–10 overall to take the Cup. Things got worse when McGee retired from the club prior to the start of the 1907 season. Ottawa returned to form with the addition of Fred "Cyclone" Taylor, whose legendary rushes into the opponents' zone earned him his famous moniker. Taylor helped the Ottawa Senators (the name Silver Seven was dropped because it was deemed unlucky after the team went three years with-out winning the Stanley Cup) to their fourth Cup win in 1909 and again in 1911. The Cup would change hands several times before Ottawa once again got a chance to bring the trophy back to the nation's capital, this time as part of the new National Hockey League.

The Senators were back on top for the 1919–20 season, finishing first in the standings. With Hall of Fame players such as Cy Denneny, Frank Nighbor and Jack Darragh and the superb goaltending of Clint Benedict, the boys from Ottawa would return the Cup to Parliament Hill three times in the next four years. The Senators would win one more Stanley Cup in 1927, but would lose their winning ways. The team folded before the start of the 1931–32 season, putting an end to one of the greatest franchises in hockey history.

Chapter Three

Influenza Cancels the Cup

The National Hockey League (formerly the National Hockey Association, which started in 1909, then folded in 1917 and reemerged as the NHL) returned in just its second year of operation with three teams for the start of the 1918–19 season. The Montréal Wanderers had ceased operations when their arena burned down in the league's inaugural season. A 20-game split schedule was drawn up by league officials, with the winners of each half meeting to decide the league championship, the winner of which would go on to face their Pacific Coast Hockey Association rivals to battle for the Stanley Cup. The Montréal Canadiens, led by scoring aces Newsy Lalonde and Odie Cleghorn, won the first half of the season easily, posting a record of seven wins and three losses. The Ottawa Senators took the second half in a season that was cut short by two games when the Toronto Arenas withdrew from the NHL because of financial difficulties. The league had no choice but to stage a best-of-seven series between the Senators and the Canadiens to determine the league champion. Montréal proved to have the upper hand in the playoffs, with stellar goaltending by legend Georges Vezina and the goal-scoring talents of Newsy Lalonde, taking the series four games to one.

Montréal would face the Pacific Division leaders, the Seattle Metropolitans, winners of the Stanley Cup in 1917, in alternating games played under both eastern and western rules. The Montréal Canadiens management had some reservations about making the long trip westward to meet Seattle, since the players would be tired from the long trip. As well, an influenza pandemic was sweeping the globe and could possibly affect the players, who would be in a confined space for the long journey. But concerns were swept aside given the importance of the match to the players and to the NHL, which was still struggling to survive. Attendance had dropped at games as posters and government declarations warned the public to stay away from large crowds and public places.

Despite the warnings and the threat of disease, the series got underway on March 19, with Seattle winning the first game convincingly 7–0 under their own western-style rules. The Canadiens bounced back with a 4–2 victory with the advantage of playing under eastern rules in the second game. When Seattle won the third game under western rules again, the series seemed destined to be decided by the rules of the game and not the quality of its players. But by the fourth game of the series, the two teams had gotten used to the different styles of play and battled to a 0–0 tie. In the fifth game, Seattle took a 3–0 lead early in the game, though defenseman Joe Hall left the ice during play, complaining that he was dizzy, tired and feverish. Newsy Lalonde came to the rescue of his teammates and scored 2 goals to give the Canadiens a 4–3 comeback victory in overtime and a second chance at taking the Cup in the final game slated for April 1, 1919.

Everything came to a grinding halt when several players began exhibiting flu-like symptoms and were sent to the hospital. It was confirmed that they had indeed contracted the dreaded influenza virus. Among the unlucky players to fall ill were defenseman Billy Coutu, manager Georges Kennedy, Jack Macdonald, Newsy Lalonde and defenseman Joe Hall, who later died in hospital from complications brought on by the virus. The Canadiens could not put enough players on the ice, and the Stanley Cup was canceled with no winner for the first time (but not the last) in its history.

Chapter Four

The Arrival of Morenz in Montréal

Since the establishment of the National Hockey League, the Montréal Canadiens had been a mediocre team, never able to rise above the talent-filled Ottawa Senators to take the league championship. Even with legendary players such as Joe Malone, Newsy Lalonde, Odie Cleghorn and Georges Vezina, the Canadiens could not manage to win the ultimate prize. Canadiens owner Leo Dandurand, however, would not give up and continued to sign quality players that would form a solid team for the future. At the start of the 1922–23 season, he signed a small, speedy forward named Aurel Joliat, and in the off-season, he found one of the greatest players in NHL history languishing in the Ontario Hockey Association Senior League with the Stratford Indians—Howie Morenz. Known for his amazing speed and physical toughness, Morenz was a welcome addition to the aging

Canadiens team, a team that hadn't challenged for the Cup since the year the championship had been canceled because of the influenza pandemic.

With the help of Morenz, the Canadiens finished second in the overall standings, but more importantly, they beat the Ottawa Senators for the NHL championship and won the right to represent the league in the battle for the Stanley Cup. But the Canadiens would not be facing off against the winner of the Pacific Coast Hockey League (PCHL) as they had done since the NHL started. Owner Frank Patrick decided that the Canadiens would play both the winners of the PCHL, the Vancouver Millionaires, and the Western Canada Hockey League (WCHL), the Calgary Stampeders. This meant that Vancouver and Calgary would play each other in a three-game series, then the loser of this series would go on to face the Canadiens, while the winner took time to recuperate. Then the winner of that series would move on to play the winner of the first series for the right to hold the Stanley Cup. This move obviously favored the western teams, but Canadiens owner Leo Dandurand agreed to the confusing playoff schedule, confident in his team's ability to beat any other team. Luckily, the Canadiens managed to beat Vancouver (the losers of the PCHL/WCHL finals) in a rough-and-tumble two-game series that saw Vancouver goaltender Hugh Lehman play most of the two games with a broken nose after he was hit in the face by an errant stick.

For the deciding series against Calgary, Morenz was ready to prove to the Canadiens and to the other players in the league that he was someone who could win a game single-handedly if the other team wasn't careful. The first game was no contest for the Canadiens, as Morenz, Joliat and Boucher dominated the game, putting in a few goals of their own to help the Habs to a 6–1 victory. The Stampeders knew that they needed something to spark them to victory, and when a team is down, they usually go after their opponents' star players, so it was no surprise that as soon as the puck was dropped, The Stampeders went after the Canadiens' star line. Boucher, Joliat and Morenz weighed about 145 pounds each and could battle in the corners as well as anyone, but when a team was set on injuring one of them, their small builds didn't help much. Calgary was desperate to stop the Montréal Canadiens, speeding through the neutral zone and using every trick in the book to slow the Habs down, hacking, slashing, hooking and holding, but nothing seemed to work. With his team already down a pair of goals, Calgary forward Cully Wilson wanted to send a message to the Canadiens and singled out Morenz as his victim.

Wilson went after Morenz, who was trying to take the puck up-ice, and slammed the rookie hard into the boards, then landed on top of him. The attack caused a hairline fracture in Morenz's collarbone and tore the shoulder ligaments. Morenz was finished for the rest of the game, but Calgary's antics did not put the Canadiens off their game. The Habs put the game away with a third goal, and goaltender Georges Vezina did the rest by shutting out the Stampeders to secure Montréal's first Stanley Cup in the National Hockey League, just the second in their history.

Morenz scored 7 goals and 3 assists in the entire playoffs, establishing himself as the first real star in what would become a long line of Montréal Canadiens heroes. His on-ice heroics would lead the Canadiens to two more Stanley Cups in 1930 and 1931 and keep the team (and some say the NHL) afloat by bringing in legions of fans wherever he went during the Depression, a time when the franchise was struggling to remain financially viable. And when Morenz could no longer produce the way he once did, the fortunes of the Canadiens turned and would not rebound until another Habs legend rocketed the team to success in the 1940s.

Chapter Five

"Silver Fox" to the Rescue

Whenever sports stories are told about a famous player or an amazing achievement, they tend to be romanticized and glorified to the point where the people involved become somewhat larger than the actual truth of the tale. However, when the story of the 1928 Stanley Cup finals between the New York Rangers and the Montréal Maroons is recounted, the truth is, in this case, stranger than fiction.

The 1927–28 season saw the Montréal Canadiens and the Montréal Maroons lead in the NHL standings and on the score sheet. Howie Morenz and Aurel Joliat finished first and second as the leading scorers for the Canadiens, and Nels Stewart took top honors for the Maroons with 27 goals, making his team easy favorites to take home the Stanley Cup. In the American division, the New York Rangers were edged out by the Boston Bruins but bounced back in the quarter- and semifinals to beat the Pittsburgh Pirates and the Bruins. Advancing to the Stanley Cup finals, they would face off against a tough Maroons squad that had just defeated the high-scoring Montréal Canadiens in a nail-biter of a series.

The Rangers, led by the coaching of hockey legend Lester Patrick, had a powerful scoring lineup, with players such as Bun Cook, Frank Boucher and Bill Cook. When they were added to a solid defensive core with Ivan "Ching" Johnson (weighing in at 210 pounds, he was a formidable obstacle in front of the net) and the goaltending of Lorne Chabot, the Rangers had a team that could match the offensive and break the defensive talents of the Maroons as long as every player stayed healthy.

Before things could even get started, the Rangers were handed their first obstacle on their road to the Cup. Madison Square Garden, it seems, was a popular venue, and with the circus in town at the time of the playoffs, the Rangers were forced to find a new arena for their home games, seeing that the circus was the bigger draw. As general manager and head coach, Lester Patrick had the option of having the team play its home games in either Boston or Detroit, but instead he chose the larger ice surface of the Montréal Forum because it favored his quick skaters over the slower, more defense-oriented Maroons.

The series did not start out the way Patrick had hoped. The Maroons potted goals in the second and third periods of the first game, while Clint Benedict stopped every single shot that came his way, for the 2–0 victory before their home crowd. Going into the second game, Patrick knew his team would have to get men in front of Benedict, because if he saw the puck coming, there was no way he would miss the save. Benedict had only allowed, on average, 1 goal per game in the play-offs and wasn't about to start letting the Rangers ruin his record.

For the second game, Patrick knew his team had to come out playing hard. The Maroons had excellent scoring power, but it was the defense and goaltending of Clint Benedict that the Rangers needed to beat to win the game. With the usual fanfare, the game got underway, and Patrick put his best defensive line against Montrèal's Nels Stewart line, hoping to keep the game close and allow the Rangers scoring line to do their job. All was going according to plan when fate intervened and made this series and this game in particular one to remember.

At just the four-minute mark of the first period, Maroons star Nels Stewart broke into the

Rangers zone and let loose a cannon of a shot that struck Rangers goaltender Lorne Chabot in the eye. Chabot hit the ice unconscious and bleeding profusely. As paramedics put Chabot onto a stretcher and rushed him to the hospital, Patrick was left to deal with the fact that he had no goaltender to replace Chabot for the rest of the game.

At a time in the league when teams only dressed one goaltender, Patrick was faced with the dilemma of replacing Chabot with another player or forfeiting the game. Patrick knew that Ottawa Senators goaltender Alec Connell was watching the game, and he immediately sent a request to the Maroons bench that the Rangers be allowed to use Connell in place of Chabot, since they had no backup goaltender. Maroons manager Eddie Girard fired back a response refusing to let Connell or any other person not under contract to the Rangers to replace Chabot in goal. Girard's polite denial to Patrick's request ended with the question: "If you need a goalkeeper, why the hell doesn't Lester play?"

Girard hadn't been born yesterday. Alec Connell was one of the best goaltenders in the league, posting 15 shutouts during the regular season and only allowing just over 1 goal per game, with a 1.24 average. Goals were hard enough to come by with Chabot in nets, so allowing one of the best shutout goaltenders into a Stanley Cup game would be a foolish move on Girard's part.

Patrick was left with very few options. He either had to dress one of his forwards or forfeit the game and hand the Maroons the easy win. With one last defiant glare at the Maroons bench, Patrick made a decision that he thought he would never have to make, but one that would go down in history as one of the most exciting moments in hockey.

With great hesitation, Patrick started putting on Chabot's sweaty pads. At the age of 44, Lester Patrick, coach and manager of the New York Rangers, was going to play in goal during a Stanley Cup game. Once the Rangers realized what Patrick was doing, they all tried to talk him out of it, but the stubborn old hockey veteran could not be stopped from playing. When he was much younger and in better shape, he had taken up the position between the posts whenever his team had needed him, but now his movements weren't quite as quick, and many on the Rangers bench wondered if the old "Silver Fox" would be able to make it through the game, let alone stop any shots.

To the shock of everyone in the stands, and especially Eddie Girard on the Maroons bench, Patrick skated out onto the ice and took his position. After Patrick got in a couple of stretches and a few practice shots, the referees readied for the faceoff. Playing with a renewed sense of purpose, the Rangers defense took it upon themselves to keep the Maroons as far away from their coach as possible. But no matter how hard they tried, Montrèal's offense still managed to get a few shots on net, yet Patrick managed to close out the first and second periods with the score still tied at zero apiece.

One can only guess at what was said between periods in the Rangers' dressing room, but the Rangers came back out onto the ice with the goal of winning the game for their coach, the man who had risked everything to keep them in the game. Patrick got the response he wanted from his team when Bill Cook scored on the Maroons only 20 seconds into the third period. Patrick wouldn't get his shutout, however, because at 14:20 of the third period, Nels Stewart broke past the defense and lifted the puck over the sprawled-out Rangers goaltender, scoring the tying goal that sent the game into overtime.

For the overtime period, the Rangers redoubled their efforts so that their coach's sacrifice would not be in vain. They could see the tired look in Patrick's eyes and wanted to end the game as quickly as they could. It took just seven minutes into overtime for Frank Boucher to split the Montréal defense, turn Benedict inside out and score the game-winning goal. The moment the goal hit the back of the net, Patrick let out a great sigh of relief and braced himself for the mob of Rangers flying off the bench to congratulate him. In the end, Patrick had stopped 17 of 18 shots on goal—not a bad effort for a 44-year-old coach. For the next game, Patrick hung up his pads and any illusions of playing again and called up a minor league goalie to replace Chabot. Although they lost that game, Chabot would return to help his team win games four and five to lead the Rangers to their first-ever Stanley Cup championship.

Despite his illustrious career as a player and a coach, Lester Patrick, the Silver Fox, will always be remembered as the middle-aged coach who came off the bench, played in goal and helped his team win a Stanley Cup game.

Chapter Six

Almost Decided by a Coin Toss

Playing in the Stanley Cup playoffs is the ultimate goal of every player in the National Hockey League. Competing teams battle hard all season for even the smallest chance to win Lord Stanley's silver Cup and would not trade that chance for anything. The playoffs are the proving grounds for the eventual winner of the Stanley Cup, and normally players will do anything to get there. This is usually what happens, but sometimes in sport, things don't go in the direction that everyone expects, which was exactly the case when the Boston Bruins met the Toronto Maple Leafs in the 1933 playoff semifinals.

The Bruins and the Maple Leafs were the two top teams from the Canadian and American divisions, and neither team was about to make the series easy for their opponent. Proof of this came in the first game in Boston, when after three periods of solid play, the teams went into over-time tied 1–1. Boston eventually put the game away in the first overtime, period on a goal by defensive stalwart Eddie Shore, but the rhythm of the series had been set and neither Boston goal-tender Tiny Thompson nor Toronto goalie Lorne Chabot were giving up any easy goals. Games two and three were almost exact carbon copies of the first game, both going into overtime, with Toronto winning game two and Boston game three. Toronto tied the series up in game four with an uncharacteristic 5–3 victory, setting the stage for the final and deciding game of the series. Neither team was going to back down and let the other walk away with the series and an automatic berth in the Stanley Cup finals.

Maple Leaf Gardens was buzzing with excite-ment before the start of game five. The fans had been treated to a tough but very close series filled with excitement and hard-hitting action, and game five would be no different. The Leafs started the game on the offensive, with Busher Jackson and Joe Primeau leading the attacks on Boston goaltender Cecil "Tiny" Thompson. But the not-so-tiny goalie held the Leafs at bay with some clutch saves to keep his team in the hunt. Boston eventually regrouped and took over con-trol of the play in the second period, with for-wards Marty Barry and Nels Stewart leading the rushes, backed up by the reliable defense of Eddie Shore. Toronto mounted a stingy defense, with guards Red Horner and King Clancy not letting any Bruins near Chabot. Throughout the second and the third periods, the action never let up, but still the deadlock held. As the two teams went into their dressing rooms at the end of regulation time, there was a sense in the building that the game might never end if play continued in the same fashion.

The teams went into the first overtime period with still no goals scored. They played a physical game in the corners and kept the offense to a minimum, but on occasion there were a few fast breaks. Both goaltenders stood on their heads to keep their respective teams' Stanley Cup hopes alive. Then came the second, third, fourth and fifth overtime periods with the exact same results. After a total of 160 minutes of hockey, neither team had yet put a puck in the net! Amazingly, most of the fans stayed through the whole game but were now looking tired and worn out by the hockey marathon. The players also started to slow down on the ice, and their body checks did not seem to have that same hard crunch when the players hit the boards.

League president Frank Calder happened to be at the game that night and was getting just as tired as everybody else in the building, but he refused the suggestion to stop the game and continue it on another day. Searching for a solution to the never-ending game, Calder suggested a few radical ideas. His strangest suggestion was to remove both goaltenders from their nets and play until the first person scored. However, this idea was quickly shot down because it gave the win to whomever could get the first lucky shot on net. Calder must have been a betting man, because his next suggestion was to have the game decided by the toss of a coin. But when the fans got wind of the plan, they booed mercilessly until Calder relinquished and let the game proceed into the sixth overtime period. At 1:50 AM, just four minutes into the sixth overtime, Toronto's Ken Doraty put everyone out of their misery when he poked the puck past Bruins netminder Tiny Thompson for the game- and series-winning goal.

The Toronto Maple Leafs went on to face the New York Rangers for the Stanley Cup but lost the best-of-five series in four games, unable to match the offensive talents of the Rangers, most likely because the Leafs were just too tired.

Chapter Seven

Mister "Sudden Death"

For the 1939 Stanley Cup playoffs, the National Hockey League decided to change the format of the playoffs, adding two best-of-seven series to be played between the two top teams for the semifinals and then the Stanley Cup final series. The opening semifinal series saw the two top teams from the regular season, the Boston Bruins and the New York Rangers face off in the first best-of-seven series starting at Madison Square Garden to decide who would go into the Stanley Cup series.

Boston's rookie goaltender Frank Brimsek, who had replaced the aging Tiny Thompson, had earned himself the nickname "Mr. Zero" after he shutout opposing teams in six of the first seven games he played in the NHL, and he wasn't about to give the Rangers any opportunities in the playoffs. The Rangers had the second-best goaltender during the season in Dave Kerr, and they had the firepower to be able to rattle the rookie Boston netminder's cage. Barring any unforeseen breakdown, the series promised to be physical, fast and tight in scoring—all the ingredients for entertaining hockey.

The first game was a perfect indication of how the rest of the series was to play out. After a full 60 minutes of back-and-forth action, the Bruins and the Rangers went into overtime, each team hoping to take the first game and the momentum of the series. However, neither team backed down from the challenge, and both goaltenders kept the fans at the Garden on the edge of their seats with some spectacular saves. It wasn't until the third overtime period that Boston rookie Mel Hill put the winning goal past Dave Kerr to take the first game. The same thing happened in the second game, but this time Hill scored the winning goal in the first overtime period to put the Bruins in a good position to sweep the Rangers out of the playoffs. In the third game, it was Boston's famed "Kraut Line" (so called because they were all from the mainly German town of Kitchener, Ontario) of Woody Dumart, Milt Schmidt and Bobby Bauer that took control of the game and led the Bruins to a 4–1 victory and a 3–0 stranglehold on the series.

The Rangers, however, did not give up easily, taking the fourth and fifth games with 2–1 victories and then silencing their critics with a 3–1 victory to tie the series and send it into a seventh and deciding match in Boston. Providing a perfect end to the series, the game went into a third overtime period, again with the score tied at 1–1. Just eight minutes into the period, Boston's Mel Hill took a pass from Bill Cowley and snapped the shot into the net for the game- and series-winning goal. The one-time Rangers reject had now earned himself the nickname Mel "Sudden Death" Hill. The Stanley Cup finals weren't particularly thrilling, as Boston, backed by Vezina and Calder Trophy–winning goaltender Frank Brimsek, easily handled the Toronto Maple Leafs in five games for their second Stanley Cup in franchise history.

Chapter Eight

Toronto Takes the Hard Road

At the end of the 1941–42 season, the New York Rangers were on top of the league with 60 points thanks to high-scoring forwards such as Bryan Hextall, Lynn Patrick and Phil Watson. Close behind in second place, the Maple Leafs would face off against the high-scoring Rangers in the first round of the playoffs. All the sportswriters predicted an easy victory for New York given their firepower and the fact that just two years earlier the almost identical lineup had won the Stanley Cup. But as history has often proved, the pundits got it wrong, and the Rangers were eliminated by the Leafs in a convincing six games. While the Leafs disposed of the Rangers, the Detroit Red Wings came out of the preliminary rounds victorious and went on to face Toronto after defeating the Montréal Canadiens and the Boston Bruins.

Toronto was delighted to have the Red Wings as their opponent. Detroit had finished the regular season with a losing record of 19–25 and seemed worn out after two difficult series in the playoffs. All the papers in Toronto predicted an easy win for the Leafs, as did many of the players in the dressing room before the start of game one. Detroit had some firepower in Don Grosso and Sid Abel, but the defense and goaltender Johnny Mowers had struggled throughout the season. The gambling types had Toronto as 8–5 favorites to take the series in convincing fashion. Aware of the gap between his team and the Maple Leafs, Detroit coach Jack Adams knew the Red Wings had one advantage over Toronto.

"We may not have the greatest hockey club in the world, but it's a club that's loaded with fighting heart," Adams proudly exclaimed. "If there's anything that wins hockey championships, it's just that."

The Red Wings came out fighting, just like their coach had promised, and checked the Leafs into submission. The Leafs' star line would barely have time to touch the puck before a Red Wings player smashed them into the boards. Detroit's best forward, Don Grosso, put his team on the scoreboard just two minutes into the game. The Leafs were obviously rattled by the Red Wings' strategy and could not mount a decent offense. Somehow they still managed to score two goals, but it wasn't enough. Don Grosso put the game away in the third period with his second goal of the game. The score at the sound of the buzzer was 3–2, and the Leafs felt lucky to have kept the game so close.

After the game, Toronto coach Hap Day tried to explain what had happened. "There's nothing wrong with our club physically. It's a question whether or not we've got the stuff that champions are made of. That wasn't hockey out there— it was a fair display of hoodlumism, Detroit's stock in trade. But we've got to adjust ourselves to the Kitty-bar-the-door tactics if we're going to win the Cup."

In the Detroit dressing room, things were very different. While celebrating their victory, the players were interrupted by several Detroit faithful—a group of fans who had raised money because they felt that their boys should be rewarded after putting up such a fight to win the game.

Game two was no different. The Leafs could not mount any significant opposition to Detroit's heavy hitters and lost the game 4–2. Detroit was overflowing with confidence, while the Leafs were left searching for answers.

"We're still in the league, I guess," Wings coach Jack Adams mocked. "We out-fought them, out-hustled them and should have beat them 7–3."

Detroit power forward Sid Abel echoed the coach's confidence by stating: "Those Leafs will know they've had their hides blistered when they get through this series."

If Toronto did not beat the Red Wings in the third game, it would be almost impossible for them to come back from such a deficit. No other team had done it since the league had adopted the best-of-seven series format. The Leafs came out strong in game three and scored 2 quick goals from Lorner Carr in under a minute, but the celebrations did not last long, as Detroit came back with 2 quick goals of their own to tie the game before the first period was finished. It got worse for Toronto in the second and third periods, as Detroit put the game away with 3 more unanswered goals to take the game 5–2. The Leafs were at a loss to explain what was happening on the ice.

"Detroit is unbeatable," said Toronto goaltender Turk Broda, obviously frustrated at his team's inability to solve the Red Wings problem. "They're too hot and they can't seem to do anything wrong."

Hap Day needed something to shake his team up if they were going to have any chance of winning at least one game. Day decided to bench veterans Bucko McDonald and Gord Drillion, who were having a good playoff series but weren't producing against the Red Wings' defensive system. Day replaced them with the fresh legs of Bob Goldham and Don Metz. Everything seemed to be going in the wrong direction—at the midway point of the second period of game four, the Red Wings had taken the lead 2–0 and looked poised to sweep the series in front of the home crowd. All they had to do was hold the lead.

Toronto had other ideas, however, and quickly tied the game before the end of the second period. Detroit would score the first goal in the third period, but Toronto got two more from Syl Apps and Nick Metz to take the game 4–3 and earn another shot at the series. Although the game was filled with action, the best was saved for the last two minutes. Frustrated at not being able to finish the game or maybe just mad at the referee for a perceived bias during the game, Red Wing Eddie Wares directed a volley of verbal assaults at referee Mel Harwood, who promptly handed him a 10-minute misconduct penalty. Just a short time later, Harwood spotted Detroit with too many men on the ice and whistled the play dead. When Don Grosso was called out to serve the two-minute infraction, he skated to the penalty box, stopped for a second to think about his next move and skated over to Harwood, dropping his stick and gloves in front of the referee in disgust. When the final buzzer sounded, all hell broke lose. Steaming mad at the sudden turn of events, Detroit coach Jack Adams jumped onto the ice and headed straight for Harwood, who was settling the final game stats in the penalty box, and pounced on the unsuspecting referee. While Harwood and the portly Adams traded haymakers, Detroit fans took it upon themselves to attack the linesmen. They nearly got to league president Frank Calder, but a group of policemen whisked him away before the mob had a chance to vent their anger. When everything was cleared up and cooler heads had reviewed the situation, Adams was given a fine and suspended indefinitely. Adams, in his oh-so-colorful manner, refused to be held back.

"They can't keep me out of Maple Leaf Gardens. I'll buy my way into the place," he said defiantly.

Game five was the turning point in the series. Detroit tried to beat the Maple Leafs into submission as in the previous games, but Toronto simply outskated them on every level. The Leafs finished the game with a 9–3 victory and a renewed sense that they could actually win the Cup.

After a penalty-laden game five, game six was extremely tame, without one penalty called during the whole game. Detroit was playing Toronto's style of game now and lost 3–0 after a brilliant performance by Leafs goalie Turk Broda, who turned aside all 32 Red Wing shots, setting the stage for game seven.

Some 16,218 fans jammed into Maple Leaf Gardens on April 18, hoping to see the Leafs mark their place in the history books and win the Stanley Cup by coming back from a 3–0 series deficit. Over the roar of the crowd, the first whistle could barely be heard as the referee dropped the puck for the opening faceoff. The Leafs fans quickly fell silent, when at the 1:44 mark of the second period, Detroit's Syd Howe scored to put the Wings in the lead. Nervous tension built up in the arena, as the rest of the second period went by without a goal from the Leafs, but the crowd erupted to life again in the third period when Sweeney Schriner tipped in a shot from the point to tie the game. Toronto took the lead on a goal by Pete Langelle and sealed Detroit's fate with a second goal from Schriner.

As the clock slowly ran down, Jack Adams bitterly accepted his fate. "Hap did a great job.

Toronto deserved to win, I guess," added Adams. "But I think they were a little bit lucky."

As the buzzer sounded, the Maple Leafs piled onto the ice and graciously shook the hands of the Red Wings players. It had been a tough series, one in which both teams were left with an equal number of cuts and bruises, but only Toronto was able to hold Lord Stanley's Cup high above their heads. They went down into the record books as the only champions ever to come back from a 3–0 series deficit to win the Cup.

Chapter Nine

The Maple Leafs' Most Famous Goal

The Red Wings were the story of the 1950–51 regular season, registering the first-ever 100-point season. Gordie Howe led the league in scoring, and rookie netminder Terry Sawchuk made his name known around the NHL, playing in all of the team's 70 games and recording 11 shutouts and a goals-against average of 1.99. Going into the playoffs, Detroit was the odds-on favorite to win the Cup, but Montréal, led by Maurice Richard, took the first two games of the semifinal series in quadruple and triple overtime. Detroit never recovered from the losses, and the Red Wings were eliminated in six games.

The Toronto Maple Leafs played the fourth-place Boston Bruins and easily beat them in five games, setting up a meeting between two of the strongest rivals in all of sports. Toronto was the better team during the regular season, finishing 30 points ahead of the Canadiens, but Montréal was riding high after they upset the Red Wings, and they weren't about to let the Leafs walk away with the Cup. The stage was set for one of the most unique and dramatic Stanley Cup finals in hockey history.

The legend of the rivalry between the two teams from Montréal and Toronto had already been firmly established through decades of battling for hockey supremacy in Canada. However, this series would take the legend to new heights and become part of hockey history.

Game one started out on the wrong foot for the Montréal Canadiens when, just 15 seconds into the game, Sid Smith scored, sending the fans that night at Maple Leaf Gardens onto their feet. Both teams traded goals back and forth, so when the third-period buzzer finally sounded, the game was tied up at 2–2. Though there were a few scoring chances in the early stages of extra time, both Montréal goaltender Gerry McNeil and Toronto's Turk Broda turned away all the difficult shots. Toronto's Sid Smith, who had opened the scoring, closed the game when he shoved the puck in the net on a backhand at 5:51 of extra time. Overtime was something that both teams would have to get used to in the next few days.

The second game of the series was another tight, high-pressure, hard-hitting affair that remained anybody's to win as momentum shifted evenly through the game. The Canadiens got on the board in the first period with a goal from Paul Masnick, and they seemed to have the game in hand when center Billy Reay put the Habs ahead by two on a setup from Richard. Usually when a visiting team goes ahead by 2 goals, it tends to take the crowd out of the game, but the Leafs fans at the Gardens that night did not let up for one moment and were rewarded with late second-period and third-period goals to send the game into overtime. This time, the winning goal came off the stick of a Montréal Canadien.

The Habs wanted the victory so as not to fall two games behind in the series, and they came out flying in the overtime period. Montréal got the first few good chances and clinched it when defenseman Doug Harvey coolly made his way through center ice and shot a tape-to-tape pass to Maurice Richard, who had gotten in behind the defense. Turk Broda came out of his crease to stop the shot, but Richard found a hole and blasted the puck home for the winner. The series was now tied as the teams headed down Highway 401 for the next two games at the Montréal Forum.

For game three, Toronto coach Joe Primeau decided at the last minute to replace veteran goaltender Turk Broda with rookie Al Rollins for the remainder of the series, gambling that youth would triumph over experience. It didn't seem like such a wise decision to change goaltenders when Maurice Richard popped in a juicy rebound with only 2:18 gone in the first period. Primeau, however, stood by his rookie goalie and was not disappointed. The youngster kept the Canadiens off the score sheet long enough for his team to tie the game and yet again send it into overtime. Less than five minutes had passed in the first overtime period when Toronto's Ted Kennedy blasted the winning goal past McNeil from a difficult angle to take a 2–1 series lead.

The fourth game was almost a carbon copy of game one, with both Toronto's Smith and Montréal's Richard opening the scoring. But this time, it was Harry Watson who slapped the puck into the net in overtime to give the Leafs a 3–1 lead in the series and the momentum going into the fifth game at Maple Leaf Gardens.

Toronto had a definite advantage going into game five. After a hard-fought playoff run, several of the Canadiens' key players were nursing injuries. Bernie "Boom Boom" Geoffrion was out with a sore knee, and filling out the injury list was sturdy winger Calum MacKay. They still had the

Rocket, but he couldn't win the Stanley Cup by himself, though that didn't stop him from trying.

Gerry McNeil kept the Canadiens alive for the first half of game five, pulling off some spectacular saves, until the Rocket scored a highlight-reel goal while carrying Toronto defenseman Jim Thomson on his back. The Canadiens attempted to stem the Leafs' rushes with some heavy physical play but seemed to have the wind knocked out of them when Canadiens forward Bob Dawes missed a check on Ted Kennedy and suffered a compound fracture to his right leg. Montréal kept battling and got a shot past Rollins on a screen shot to give the Habs the lead. They lost it with seconds remaining on the clock after a mad scramble in front of McNeil when Sloan picked up the garbage goal to send the game into overtime. (Sounds familiar!)

It took only 2 minutes and 53 seconds for the game to come to an end. The Leafs managed to work the puck into the Montréal end, battling hard in the corners for control. Howie Meeker got control of the puck behind the net and spotted defenseman Bill Barilko streaking in from the blue line for an open shot. Meeker threaded the puck through the action and hit Barilko with a pass. Barilko slapped the puck past a sprawledout Gerry McNeil for the game- and Stanley

Cup–winning goal. The Toronto Maple Leafs stormed off the bench and lifted Barilko onto their shoulders as the crowd roared their approval.

Coach Joe Primeau had told Barilko all year that the slapshot was a fad in hockey and that it would never become a useful tool, but now Barilko was the one with the final word. "I told you it was a deadly shot," Barilko yelled to Primeau in the dressing room.

Maple Leafs general manager Conn Smythe sang the praises of their young hero after the game: "At times he was such a problem, I wanted to send him down to Pittsburgh, but thank God we kept him."

Years later, Habs goaltender Gerry McNeil looked back at the series on a positive note. "I am proud of what we achieved. I mean, that was something—knocking out the Cup champion [Detroit Red Wings] in the semifinals and then five straight overtime games in the finals. We achieved something special," said McNeil fondly.

But the celebrations would not last long. Just a few weeks after winning his first Stanley Cup, Barilko and his friend Dr. Henry Hudson boarded a plane and headed north for a week of fishing on the Seal River. After a short refueling stop, the two friends took off for their final destination but were never heard from again. A search-and-rescue team was immediately sent into the dense forests where the plane was last reported seen, but after exhaustive land and air searches, no trace of the plane or Barilko and Hudson could be found. It wasn't until 11 years later, in 1962, that the mystery of Bill Barilko's disappearance was finally solved when a plane passing over a remote section of forest near Cochrane, Ontario, spotted a piece of metal shining through the growth. When people went in to get a closer look, they found the plane that Barilko and Hudson were last seen in and two skeletons still strapped in their seats.

Even stranger than Barilko's disappearance was the fact that the Leafs didn't win another Stanley Cup until the year his body was discovered. His jersey still hangs from the rafters at the new home of the Maple Leafs as a reminder of the life and all-too-brief career that the 24-year-old defenseman left behind when he disappeared that summer in 1951.

Chapter Ten

Eight in a Row!

Just as the Montréal Canadiens dominated the late 1950s, the Detroit Red Wings were the best team in the National Hockey League from 1949 to 1955. They had finished first in the division seven years in a row, a feat not likely ever to be repeated, and had a team filled with future Hall of Fame members. At the start of the 1951–52 season, the Red Wings had everything in place for a great season. Gordie Howe was healthy, and Terry Sawchuk was coming off a rookie year in which he had won the Calder Trophy. Add to that the steady, rough play of Ted Lindsay and Sid Abel, and Detroit was primed to lead the way through the regular season.

With everything firmly in place, the Red Wings finished the regular season comfortably on top of the league with their second straight 100-plus-point season and were the favorites going into the playoffs to walk away with the

Stanley Cup. They opened the semifinals against third-place team and defending Stanley Cup champions, the Toronto Maple Leafs.

Toronto barely had time to realize what was happening before Detroit, or better yet Terry Sawchuk, had built a 2–0 series lead by shutting the Leafs out twice. Detroit breezed to a 6–2 victory in game three and took game four with ease, with Terry Sawchuk doing most of the heavy lifting, for a 3–1 victory.

In the meantime, the Canadiens battled it out in a rough seven-game series against the Boston Bruins. The Bruins-Habs series saw one of the most famous goals in NHL history scored by Maurice Richard. In game seven, Richard missed most of the play because of a concussion he suffered as a result of being hit in the head in the first period. Richard was sitting in the dressing room, barely able to focus, when head coach Dick Irvin entered and told Richard to get back on the ice and win the game. With a bandage over his left eye and a terrible pain in his head, Richard got back out on the ice and scored on an end-to-end rush that sent the fans at the Forum to their feet for a four-minute ovation. Richard had broken the tie, and the Canadiens took the final game by a score of 3–1. In the dressing room after the game, Richard collapsed and broke into tears. Like a true competitor, he had done what the coach asked, but it had taken everything out of him.

The Canadiens had won their semifinal series but came out so battered and so tired that the Red Wings had the upper hand in the finals. The Canadiens had no energy left and only scored 2 goals on Terry Sawchuk in the entire series as the Red Wings swept the Canadiens in four straight. Sawchuk finished the playoffs with a record eight straight wins, recording a goals-against average of 0.63, only 5 goals against and an amazing four shutouts. No goaltender since has ever come close to achieving those kinds of numbers. Detroit were the undisputed, uncontested champions of the National Hockey League for the fifth time in their history, and no team was able to match their eight consecutive victories with no losses until the Montréal Canadiens in the 1960 Stanley Cup playoffs.

Chapter Eleven

The Cup That Should Have Been

The 1950s belonged to the Montréal Canadiens. At the beginning of the decade, the Canadiens were a mediocre team that struggled their way through the playoffs and only made it farther because of hard work and the clutch play of their star player, Maurice "Rocket" Richard. But as the Canadiens moved on from their disappointing loss to the Toronto Maple Leafs in the 1951 Stanley Cup finals, they were quickly becoming the team of the future. Maurice Richard was always a threat when he was on the ice, and he was now joined by young up-and-comers such as Bernie Geoffrion, goaltender Jacques Plante, Dickie Moore and Jean Beliveau, among others. Together they would eventually form the best team ever to play the game of hockey. The Detroit Red Wings' Gordie Howe, Terry Sawchuk and Ted Lindsay had been thorns in the Canadiens' side from the start of the 1950s.

The Red Wings played a tough game and deserved every single win they got on the ice, but when the Canadiens and the Red Wings met in the 1955 Stanley Cup playoffs, the Red Wings had a slight advantage over the Habs that would eventually lead to Detroit's second Cup victory in a row.

The Red Wings got their advantage earlier in the season, when the actions of one Montréal Canadiens player set in motion a series of events that would mark the game of hockey and the city of Montréal for years to come.

Since his arrival in the National Hockey League in the early 1940s, Maurice Richard had remained a controversial figure. Being a French-Canadian star in an English-dominated sport forced him to face a unique set of challenges and obstacles. From the time he scored his first goal with the Canadiens, Maurice Richard became a target in the league. He was the Canadiens' number one player, and all the tough players across the league would challenge him every chance they got. But Richard was never one to back down from a fight, and he taught many lessons to young players who tried to make their mark in the NHL by going after a superstar. Although Richard could handle himself on the ice in any situation, he long believed that he wasn't accorded fair treatment by the referees, and especially league president Clarence Campbell, when it came to the protection of the league's best players. Players such as Gordie Howe, Ted Kennedy and Bill Mosienko were all looked after and treated fairly, but Richard, a French Canadian, knew he was a marked man on the ice. Resigned to his fate, Richard continued his high quality of play and fought back whenever challenged, leading to many confrontations with the media, management and most of all NHL president Clarence Campbell.

The problems between Richard and Campbell began to heat up at the beginning of the 1954–55 season. Richard had long been an outspoken critic of Campbell and had aired his views in a local French-language newspaper, attacking Campbell personally and professionally by saying that he was a "dictator" who openly cheered against the Canadiens because they were a predominantly French-Canadian team. For exercising his right to free speech, Richard was fined $1000 and forced to publicly apologize if he wanted to play again. Although his outspoken nature earned him many enemies, in Québec, Richard was lauded as a hero for standing up to his English bosses. He could do no wrong in the eyes of Canadiens' fans, to Campbell's great consternation.

"For every $250 I fined him, Québec business-men would send him $1000," said Campbell.

The tension finally came to a head on the night of March 13, 1955, when the Montréal Canadiens played the Boston Bruins at Boston Garden. The Bruins were playing a very rough game, and as usual, Maurice Richard was the target of much of their aggression. For most of the game, Richard was hooked, grabbed, slashed and tripped—the opposition used just about any means necessary to slow him down. The violence came to a head when Richard collided with Bruins defenseman Hal Laycoe. As Richard fell to the ice, his stick caught Laycoe on the head and cut him. Furious at the sight of blood, Laycoe swung his stick at Richard and caught him on top of the head, opening a cut that bled profusely. When he saw his own blood, Richard lost his cool. Richard's trademark glare burned with revenge as both players tried to take each other's heads off in a flurry of stick swinging.

Seeing that things were getting out of control, linesman Cliff Thompson jumped in to try and stop the fighting. Thompson tried to restrain Richard from getting at Laycoe, but the Rocket was so mad that he kept breaking free to continue his pursuit of Laycoe. Frustrated that his efforts to restrain Richard were having no effect, the linesman grabbed Richard again, but this time Thompson pinned Richard's arms behind his back so he couldn't break free so easily. Richard yelled for Thompson to let him go, but the linesman held firm. At this point, Laycoe saw that Thompson was tying up Richard and proceeded to punch the Rocket. Canadiens defenseman Doug Harvey came to his teammate's rescue and knocked the linesman off Richard. Fuming with rage, the Rocket turned around and punched Thompson square in the face twice.

"He wouldn't listen," said Richard after the game. "That's why I hit him."

Richard knew the outcome wouldn't be good, but he still had some hope that things would work out. However, when word finally came down from NHL president Clarence Campbell that Richard was to be suspended for the remainder of the season, including the playoffs, it started a series of events that would make both hockey and Montréal history.

Local anger was echoed by the press, who blared their discontent at the suspension in large black print across the front page of almost every paper in town. Campbell was not a very popular person in the eyes of most Montréalers, who took the suspension as a slight against the Canadiens and French people in general. The social and economic gap between the English and the French in Montréal at that time was a major source of tension between the "two solitudes," and the Richard affair brought strong emotions to the surface. Still, despite threatening phone calls from Richard supporters and warnings from the Montréal police, Campbell wanted to attend a scheduled game at the Montréal Forum between the Canadiens and the Detroit Red Wings.

On March 17, 1955, the Canadiens were set to play an important game against the Red Wings, who were fighting for the top spot in the division. The mood inside the Forum was tense as the game got underway and Campbell slowly approached his seat. Outside the arena, an angry mob of fans had gathered, chanting slogans denouncing Campbell with increasing volume.

Halfway through the game, it became apparent that the fans were not so interested in what was happening on the ice and were concentrating on venting their anger at the NHL president. Everything got out of control when a young man approached Campbell and punched him several times before police could intervene. As the young man was being led away, someone threw a tear-gas canister near Campbell, and everyone immediately ran for the exits. Once the angry fans from inside the Forum mixed with the angry fans outside, the situation quickly escalated into a full-scale riot. The 250 police officers on-site could do little to stem the destruction as nearly 10,000 irate Montréalers ransacked the downtown area. When the riot finally died down, over 70 people had been arrested, and the mob had caused over $100,000 in damage.

Maurice Richard went on the radio and appealed to the public for calm: "I will take my punishment and come back next year."

The Red Wings won the game that night and ended up winning the regular season championship. The Canadiens, still reeling from the riots, managed to defeat the Bruins in the semifinals and faced off against the Red Wings for the Stanley Cup. The series was a good battle between the two top teams, but the Red Wings came out the winners in game seven with a 3–1 victory. Many Montréalers, Habs fans and even Maurice Richard himself felt that the outcome of the series might have been far different had the Rocket been in the Canadiens lineup. The next year, Richard returned to the Habs and helped them to the top of the division and to the first of five consecutive Stanley Cups. Greedy? Perhaps, but it could have been six.

Chapter Twelve

The Cup Runneth Over

Although there had been dynasties before, hockey had never seen anything like the team the Montréal Canadiens put on the ice from 1955 to 1960. Through every playoff year in which they won the Stanley Cup, they never went more than six games in a series and were hard pressed to find a suitable challenger during those years. From 1945 to 1967, the National Hockey League experienced its best years. Many players stayed with the same team for their entire careers, and competition for new talent brought out the worst in many of the general managers. Signing good players to long-term contracts meant securing success for your team for years to come, and no team was better at it than the Montréal Canadiens and their general manager Frank Selke.

Taking control of the Habs in 1946, Selke sought to establish a team in Montréal that would withstand changes in the league and the inevitable challenges of having a hockey team in that city—something that was and still is no easy task. However, years under the tutelage of Conn Smythe in Toronto had prepared Selke for what needed to be done to succeed. During Selke's reign over the Montréal Canadiens, he brought in players such as Jean Beliveau, Henri Richard, Bernie Geoffrion, Dickie Moore, Doug Harvey, Jacques Plante and Bert Olmstead and Toe Blake as coach. In addition, he set up a junior system in every province (particularly in Québec), giving the Canadiens a very large and talented pool of players to choose from for years to come. This would allow the Canadiens team to sustain its veteran talent and secure a good team for the future. Selke had a keen sense for talent, which brought the Canadiens into a record 10 straight Stanley Cup finals. The team reached its pinnacle during the 1959–60 season. Out of all the players on the roster Canadiens that year, an amazing 11 would go on to become Hall of Fame inductees.

For the 1960 playoffs, the Canadiens were set to take on the third-place Chicago Blackhawks with their young scoring ace, Bobby Hull, and "Mr. Goalie," Glenn Hall, in a series that everyone suspected the Canadiens would dominate. The first two games of the series surprised the very confident Canadiens squad, but they managed to hold on for two 4–3 victories. The Canadiens would regroup, and with the help of the spectacular goaltending of Jacques Plante, they shut the Blackhawks out in the next two games to sweep the series with relative ease. This victory set the stage for the classic Montréal versus Toronto rivalry.

Toronto coach Punch Imlach tried to use the media to play mind games with the Canadiens, but the team was too experienced and too rich with talent to let any verbal jousting get in the way of another Stanley Cup. In game one, the Canadiens proved the bookies and newspapers right by taking the game easily with a score of 4–2 and got their only real challenge of the series in game two, when Toronto missed by just one goal to go down in a 2–1 defeat. That was as close as the Maple Leafs would get to winning a game in the finals. The Canadiens won game three 5–2, led by a hat trick from Phil Goyette, and then took the final game 4–0 after a brilliant performance from Jacques Plante. Before a soldout crowd at Maple Leaf Gardens, the Canadiens calmly accepted the Stanley Cup, having become old hands at celebrating.

"When you win 4–0 in four games and after four Cup titles, you don't get too excited," said Canadiens defenseman Doug Harvey.

Maurice Richard's goal in game three, his 82nd career playoff goal, proved to be the last one he would ever score. After 18 incredible seasons with the Montréal Canadiens, Maurice Richard announced his retirement.

The Canadiens remained a competitive team the following season but didn't make it back into the Stanley Cup finals until 1965, the year they won the Cup with a newer wave of Montréal Canadiens stars that would see the Habs through two more successful decades.

Chapter Thirteen

The New and Improved Blackhawks

The 1960–61 regular season ended with the Montréal Canadiens in first place yet again, and their star player that year was Bernie "Boom Boom" Geoffrion, whose pioneering of the slapshot led him to become only the second person in NHL history to score 50 goals during a season. But heading into the playoffs, the Canadiens did not look like the favorites they had been for the five previous playoff seasons.

The Chicago Blackhawks, on the other hand, had only finished in third place, but they entered the playoffs with energy and youth on their side. With young talent such as Bobby Hull, Stan Mikita, Pierre Pilote and the always-reliable goaltending of "Mr. Goalie" himself, Glenn Hall, the Blackhawks were favored to take the series. Montréal was without their top scorer, Bernie Geoffrion, who was sidelined with his leg in a cast, but the Habs still managed to take the first game by a score of 6–2 on a night when it was obvious that Glenn Hall was having a bad time. The Blackhawks came back to life in the second game, taking the match 4–3 to tie the series. The Canadiens would come back to win only one more game, as the Blackhawks simply out-played and out-hit them at every turn. With Glenn Hall shutting out Montréal in the final two games, Chicago easily took the series in six. This would be the Hawks' first appearance in the Stanley Cup finals since the Montréal Canadiens beat them in 1944. The Hawks had suffered years of bad management, and a mediocre farm system had left them without any depth in their lineup since they had last won the Cup in 1938. But then-owner Jim Norris opened his wallet and brought players to the team that gave the Hawks back some respect.

Meanwhile, thanks to some spectacular goaltending from Terry Sawchuk, the fourth-place Detroit Red Wings upset the second-place Toronto Maple Leafs in five games to move on to meet the Blackhawks for the Stanley Cup. Both teams went into the series confident that they could bring the silverware home after beating two of the top teams in the league. Both boasted an impressive lineup of goal scorers and solid goaltending. Fans were eager to see which of their favorite superstar players would come out on top at the end of the series. Gordie Howe was the grizzled veteran who could always be found among the leading scorers, while Bobby Hull was the new vision of the NHL. Big, strong and possessing the hardest slapshot at the time, Hull was always a threat on the ice.

Game one on April 6, 1961, gave the fans their answer when Hull scored 2 goals in the first period to lead the Blackhawks to a 3–2 victory. The Red Wings roared back under the goaltending of Hank Bassen, who had replaced an injured Terry Sawchuk, and won the second game 3–1, evening the series at one game apiece. They split the next two games, each team winning a game on home ice. The fifth and sixth games turned out to be the decisive games for the Blackhawks.

Before a soldout crowd packed like sardines into Chicago Stadium, the Hawks, led by the goal-scoring performances of Stan Mikita and Murray Balfour, easily took the fifth game by a final score of 6–3. The Red Wings didn't have enough energy left to stop the Blackhawk offense and were worn down even further by the steady pounding from Chicago's checking lines.

Game six was do-or-die time for the Detroit Red Wings. Head coach Jack Adams knew his team would need a miracle to beat Chicago, but he still had hope for his squad. He told his players to open up the game and take those occasional offensive chances, and the strategy paid off immediately when they scored the only goal in the first period. The Red Wings started the second period confident that they could build on their lead and take the series into game seven. Early in the second frame, the Blackhawks were called on a penalty, giving the Wings a chance to pad their lead. Concentrating around Glenn Hall's net, the Red Wings tried desperately to put the puck in, but in their eagerness, they allowed Chicago's Reggie Fleming to intercept a pass for an open breakaway straight at Detroit goaltender Bassen. Streaking towards the net, Fleming forced Bassen to commit to a save on the far side and then just slid the puck into the opposite side for the short-handed goal. A hush fell over the Detroit crowd at Olympia Stadium. After that goal, the Red Wings seemed to lose the will to win, and Chicago capitalized by scoring 4 unanswered goals to take the game 5–1 and win the Stanley Cup championship.

After the game, Jack Adams didn't have to think hard when asked why his team had lost the Cup. "We just ran out of gas," he said.

Chicago made it to the finals again in 1962, but the Toronto Maple Leafs were just too strong, and the Blackhawks to this day have yet to win another Cup (45 years and counting at the time of writing).

Chapter Fourteen

The End of the Golden Years

The 1966–67 season would be the last for the original six members from hockey's golden era before the league expanded, and the two teams that epitomized that era would face off in one of the most dramatic Stanley Cup playoffs in National Hockey League history.

Before the start of the season, Toronto head coach Punch Imlach was surrounding himself with veteran players that probably should have been on the golf course rather than in training camp, but Imlach felt that if the Leafs were to pose a threat to any other team that year, he wanted to have a group of guys with experience and the desire to win at all costs. However, Imlach was not just surrounding himself with a bunch of grizzled veterans. His lineup included multiple-Cup-winning goaltenders Terry Sawchuk and Johnny Bower, all-star defenseman-turned-forward Red Kelley, defenseman Allan

Stanley and forward Marcel Pronovost, all closing in on 40 years of age. Filling out the rest of his lineup were a few younger stars that would benefit from the veterans' experience: Frank Mahovlich, Jim Pappin, Ron Ellis and Brian Conacher.

Despite the level of talent on the team, the regular season was a stressful affair for the Leafs and especially for their coach. At one point during the season, after the team lost a string of 10 straight games, Imlach checked himself into the hospital because of stress and exhaustion. Imlach's high-pressure coaching style was replaced by that of Toronto favorite King Clancy. Things immediately turned around for the veteran squad, and the team finished in third place behind Chicago and Montréal. With Imlach out of the picture, the Maple Leafs improved their record over the next 10 games to 7–1–2 and locked in third spot at the end of the regular season. It wasn't with the greatest of finishes that they entered into the playoffs, but the team was healthy, and more importantly, they wanted to win.

For the first round of the 1967 Stanley Cup playoffs, the Leafs faced off against the high-scoring Chicago Blackhawks. The Hawks relied on offensive players such as Stan Mikita, Bobby

Hull, Kenny Wharram, a young Phil Esposito and Doug Mohns and the always-solid goaltending of Glenn Hall to be able to overwhelm their opponents with sheer offensive output. That is not to say that the Hawks lacked on defense—they had all-star Norris Trophy–winner Pierre Pilote and the large, 6'3", 205-pound frame of Doug Jarrett to stop any offensive threat the Leafs might throw at them.

The Leafs, on the other hand, were thought to be a team of washed-up veterans that had barely a chance of defeating the younger, faster, stronger Hawks team. The Leafs were confident that they could win, and Imlach knew from their previous meetings during the regular season that the Blackhawks were prone to mistakes. The Hawks of the 1960s were consistent under-achievers. They had finished at the top of the league several times and boasted a lineup that had won the scoring race seven out of nine times, but for some reason, they could never put together a consistent string of victories. The Leafs knew this, and it was Imlach's job to exploit it. But game one didn't go as planned for the Leafs. The Hawks came out fast and won the game by a score of 5–2. The second game belonged to Sawchuk, whose acrobatic saves kept his team alive long enough to hold on and win 3–1. The teams split the next two games, but Toronto seemed to have the Hawks' number. By game five, Chicago had nothing left to give and could not break Imlach's tight defensive system, so they lost both games five and six. Like the proverbial underachievers they were, the Hawks were again eliminated from the playoffs.

Bobby Hull saw one man as being responsible for their early exit: "I saw him [Terry Sawchuk] make those saves, but I still can't believe it."

But it was more than just Sawchuk. The Leafs didn't try to play the Blackhawks' style of game and stubbornly stuck to their tight defense to keep the games as close as possible. The Montréal Canadiens, meanwhile, had an easy time with the New York Rangers and swept their series in four straight games, setting up a matchup between the only two Canadian teams in the league during Canada's centennial year.

The finals were shaping up to be one of the most exciting playoffs in a long time. The Canadiens seemed on the verge of another dynasty like that of the late 1950s and had already won in 1965 and 1966 thanks to the talent of veteran players such as Jean Beliveau and Henri Richard and the youthful speed of Yvan Cournoyer and Ralph Backstrom. Rivalry between the teams had already been established through decades of intense battles, but this series would solidify the bad blood between the two cities. The divisions were many: Montréal was French, Toronto was English; Montréal played a finesse game, Toronto played a tough checking one. It would be skillful speed versus hardworking veterans.

Although the Leafs had defeated the powerful Blackhawks, sportswriters from across the country doubted whether the "Over-the-Hill Gang" could defeat the more consistent Montréal Canadiens. But this only served to inspire the Maple Leafs, who made it their mission to prove to the naysayers that they could defy everyone's expectations and at the very least give the Canadiens a run for their money. One sportswriter compared the Montréal lineup to "jet fighters" up against Toronto's slow "World War I Sopwith Camels." Montréal's main weak point came in goal. Although the Canadiens had relied on Gump Worsley for their two previous Stanley Cup championships, head coach Toe Blake decided to put rookie goaltender Rogatien Vachon in nets for the finals after he'd had an excellent end to the regular season.

Prior to game one, Imlach attempted to get under the skin of the rookie goaltender to shake him off his game. "You can tell that Junior B goaltender he won't be playing against a bunch of peashooters. When he plays against the Leafs, we'll take his head off with our first shot," taunted Imlach, but the rookie goaltender wasn't biting.

"What's the difference between stopping the puck at Thetford Mines or at the Forum?" wondered Vachon, obviously unaffected by Imlach's taunts.

All the words and posturing fell to the side once the puck was dropped for the opening face-off in game one at the Montréal Forum. Five minutes into the first period, the Leafs looked a little tentative in their forechecking and only got two scoring chances on the Canadiens goal, which Vachon took care of nonchalantly. The Canadiens opened up the scoring on a powerplay goal from Yvan Cournoyer, but just 15 seconds later, Larry Hillman scored for Toronto to tie the game. After that, it was all Montréal, led by a hat trick from Henri Richard, and the Canadiens finished the game with a decisive 6–2 victory. Afterwards, some of the Montréal players expressed surprise at how easily they had beaten the Leafs.

"I thought they would come out hitting, but they didn't," said Henri Richard.

Sawchuk had a horrible night, looking amateurish on several goals and never really finding his rhythm in nets. After the game, Sawchuk commented to reporters on his performance:

"I got one thing to say, gentlemen. I didn't have a good night."

This was definitely not the same Leafs team that had defeated the high-scoring Hawks with a tight checking game. The Canadiens had the run of the ice, and Vachon had only really been tested on a few occasions. But game two would be a different story.

After Sawchuk's poor performance, Johnny Bower would get to start in nets for the Maple Leafs for game two. This time, the Leafs played their system to perfection, keeping players such as Henri Richard and Jean Beliveau to the outside of the Toronto net with some tough checking. It wasn't all sunshine for the Leafs, however, because the Canadiens had a tough checker of their own in John Ferguson. Anytime he was on the ice, he could be found in front of Bower, making the Toronto goaltender's job a very difficult one. Several times during the game, he made a point of falling or knocking the 42-year-old Bower on the head, but the veteran goaltender wasn't fazed by the attention and stopped all 31 shots that the Canadiens sent his way. On the other end, Vachon was very busy, stopping 43 of 46 shots for the 3–0 loss. Bower again made the difference as the series moved to Toronto, where he stopped an incredible 52 shots as the Leafs went on to win game three in the second overtime on a goal from Bob Pulford. On the back of Johnny Bower, Toronto had taken a 2–1 series lead and had the Canadiens scrambling to explain why they couldn't score the important goals.

"What do we have to do to put the puck in the net?" questioned Canadiens winger Gilles Tremblay.

Things were looking brighter for the Leafs as they headed into game four confident that they could take a commanding lead in the series if their goaltending could withstand the Montréal offense. However, things took a turn for the worse when Bower's age finally caught up with him, and he pulled a muscle in the pre-game warmup. Bower was unable to play for the rest of the series, making Terry Sawchuk the goaltender that the Leafs would have to use for the remaining games. Sawchuk strapped on his pads and took his position in net for the start of the fourth game. Yet again, Sawchuk had a horrible game, looking unsure of himself on every shot. In the end, the Canadiens put six pucks into the net for a 6–2 victory.

A despondent Sawchuk commented after the game on his performance: "Sometimes you can't keep the puck out with a snowplow."

Sawchuk redeemed himself in game five with a one-goal performance, while the Canadiens' rookie netminder Rogie Vachon let in 2 soft goals and was eventually replaced by Gump Worsley. The game ended in a 4–1 Canadiens loss before a very quiet Montréal Forum crowd. Imlach's mind games with the Canadiens' rookie goalie seemed to be working, and Worsley was slated to start in the pivotal sixth game in Toronto.

The men in blue and white were taking control of the series as they had done against the Blackhawks. The Canadiens seemed perplexed over Terry Sawchuk's sudden turnaround and were unsure how they were going to beat him in game six on home ice. The Canadiens needed to turn things around quickly, and Blake tried to inspire his team with some words of encouragement.

"Home ice won't be a factor until the seventh game," said Blake, trying to bring some life back into the Canadiens' dressing room. "That's right—only in the seventh game, when we win the Cup." Blake had been around long enough to know when his team needed a boost, but deep down inside, he knew his team needed a miracle to pull off the championship.

To get anything going, the Canadiens needed their high-powered offense to start producing, but that would mean solving the Terry Sawchuk problem. The tension in Maple Leaf Gardens that night was high as the fans crowded into their seats, readying themselves for the opening face-off. To their dismay, it looked as if the Canadiens came out the hardest, peppering Sawchuk with 17 shots in the first period. But the veteran goaltender was playing up to his future Hall of Fame standard, repelling all the shots that came his way. Worsley was no slouch either, stopping the Leafs on all their shots and making one especially nice save on a Frank Mahovlich slapshot to end the first period with no points on the board.

The second period belonged to the Leafs. The "Over-the-Hill Gang" banded together and brought the crowd at Maple Leaf Gardens to their feet in the sixth minute of play, when Ron Ellis scored on a rebound shot by Red Kelly on a two-on-one break. The Leafs continued to press the Habs, sensing Montréal's weakness, and scored the eventual game winner with just 38 seconds remaining in the second period. Former Maple Leaf Dick Duff would bring the Canadiens within one, but George Armstrong's empty net goal in the last minute of play clinched the victory for the Leafs, and Toronto erupted in celebration.

Against all odds, the oldtimers had defeated the regular season's two best teams, thanks mostly to the confidence and competitive spirit given to them by their coach Punch Imlach.

"This is my most satisfying Cup," said Imlach after the game, sipping champagne out of the trophy. "Everybody said I'd never win another Cup with these old guys. Well, maybe that makes this the biggest kick of all for me, because we sure shoved it down everybody's throats. With expansion coming up, I won't be able to keep them all. But now they're going out as champs, and that's the way it should be."

Toronto would celebrate that Stanley Cup win like no other in their history. They had defied the oddsmakers and taken the Cup from one of the best teams in the game. Unfortunately for the organization, the Leafs still to this day have yet to win another Stanley Cup or even make it into another Stanley Cup final, but the memory of that glorious victory still lives in the hearts of Toronto fans everywhere.

Part II
THE NEW LEAGUE

The end of the 1967 season and the Toronto Maple Leafs' victory over the Montréal Canadiens in the Stanley Cup finals signaled the end of the golden years of hockey. The original six members of the National Hockey League hadn't changed since the Brooklyn Americans folded as the seventh team in 1942, leaving the Detroit Red Wings, Toronto Maple Leafs, Boston Bruins, Chicago Blackhawks, New York Rangers and Montréal Canadiens as the remaining six teams. Through the 1950s and 1960s, hockey's popularity grew in leaps and bounds, especially in the United States, and in order to capitalize on a greater share of the professional sports market, the NHL decided to add six more teams to the league. Among the new teams were the Philadelphia Flyers, Los Angeles Kings, St. Louis Blues, Minnesota North Stars, Pittsburgh Penguins and Oakland Seals. Some of the teams succeeded immediately, while others faded into obscurity and the pages of hockey franchise history. Over the next few decades, the face of hockey would change forever, and new dynasties would be formed in the pursuit of the same trophy that every hockey player has desired since 1893.

Chapter Fifteen

All Hail Bobby Orr!

Bobby Orr had long been touted as the next great thing in the NHL, even before he had played a single game. When he finally arrived to start the 1966 season with the Boston Bruins, he took home the Calder Trophy as the rookie of the year. The NHL had never seen a defenseman like Orr, who could move the puck with such ease and grace. With every year that passed, coaches throughout the league were faced with the problem of how they could stop Orr and his innovative end-to-end rushes. The end-to-end was nothing new in hockey, but the NHL had never seen a defenseman with the offensive-minded ability of Orr, who could change the tempo of a game on a single rush. By the start of the 1969–70 season, Bobby Orr and the rest of the Boston Bruins squad were rewriting the record books with some of the most exciting and offensive hockey the NHL had seen in years.

Orr, along with Phil Esposito, Johnny Bucyk and the goaltending of Gerry Cheevers, confounded opponents, and the Bruins finished the season tied with Chicago for top spot in the league. Another addition to the Bruins already-impressive arsenal of talent was Derek Sanderson. Sanderson was the equivalent of a Sean Avery or Darcy Tucker in today's NHL—a player who can score goals and get another team in trouble just by his presence on the ice. Sanderson was a certified agitator, always mouthing off in the media and on the ice to put the other team off their game. He could also score goals when necessary, his highest total being 29 goals in the 1970–71 season. Orr finished the regular season as the leading scorer in the league with 33 goals and 87 assists for 120 points, the first time in National Hockey League history that a defenseman had won the scoring title. With a defenseman that could score with the grace of Jean Beliveau, pass like a playmaking center and defend like the great Doug Harvey, Boston was set to go far in the playoffs. Orr was Boston's not-so-secret secret weapon. The Bruins headed into the playoffs set to take on the New York Rangers in the opening quarterfinals.

It had been 29 years since the Boston Bruins had won the Cup with Hall of Fame players such as Dit Clapper, Woody Dumart and goaltender

Frank Brimsek, and many in Boston were counting on Orr and all the future Hall of Famers on the team to lead the Bruins to victory. The Bruins took the first two games at Boston Garden easily with scores of 8–2 and 5–3. They were only interrupted on their way to the semifinals by two road losses, winning the series in six games. Boston's win resulted in Tony Esposito's Chicago Blackhawks taking on brother Phil Esposito's Bruins. Although Phil's little brother had recorded 15 shutouts during the regular season, and the Hawks had swept the Detroit Red Wings in four straight games, Tony would not have such luck against his brother and Orr. The Hawks were easily outscored in the series 20–10 in a four-game sweep. Orr had scored 8 goals in the 10 playoff games so far, leading the charge to the Stanley Cup final against two-time finals losers, the St. Louis Blues.

The St. Louis Blues were the first success story to come out of the expansion of the league in 1967. Under the guidance of rookie coach Scotty Bowman, the St. Louis Blues went from a team of veteran and rookie castoffs to being the most surprising playoff team of the late 1960s and early 1970s. Led by Phil Goyette, Red Berenson and the 1969 Vezina Trophy–winning tandem of Jacques Plante and Glenn Hall, they were very far from being the powerhouse that the Bruins were during the season. But under Bowman's coaching, St. Louis continued to surprise, so nothing was being left to chance in the final showdown.

Bowman was keenly aware of the problems facing him in the final series. "We practiced covering Bobby Orr for six hours today, but the only trouble is, we don't have a Bobby Orr to practice against," said coach Bowman when asked how his team had prepared for the series against the Bruins. "We don't stand a chance unless we stop Bobby Orr. We'll rise or fall on that strategy."

Bowman's strategy failed in the first game.

While the Blues were busy trying to keep Bobby Orr contained, the remainder of the talent-filled Bruins squad skated freely in the St. Louis zone. By the end of the game, the Bruins had scored 6 goals, while all the Blues could manage was a single point. Orr commented after the game on how much attention he was receiving from the Blues' checking lines.

"I could have gone out to lunch for all the chances I got to play," said Orr sarcastically. "So I just stayed out of things."

Scrapping his earlier strategy, Bowman told his players to concentrate less on Orr and more on playing a solid game of hockey. But the young, high-flying offense of the Bruins was too much for Bowman's team of veterans, and they easily took game two by a score of 6–2 and game three by a score of 4–1.

The Blues knew the ending was inevitable, but they wanted to finish the Stanley Cup finals with at least one win. "We got to go out fighting or we won't be able to hold our heads up," said the Blues' Jimmy Roberts.

The Blues battled in game four at Boston Garden in front of an eager bunch of Bruins fans wanting to see their team win the Cup on home ice. The Blues came out strong and gave the home crowd a scare, taking the lead in the game several times, but the Bruins came back on the strength of goals from Esposito and Bucyk to tie the game and send it into overtime.

Orr, who hadn't scored a goal the entire series against the Blues, took just 30 seconds into overtime to make history. On a Bruins rush into the Blues' zone, Derek Sanderson spotted Orr rushing to the net and caught him with a precision pass. Orr made his way in front of goaltender Glenn Hall and banged home the puck for the game-winning goal. At the same moment that the puck crossed the line, Orr was tripped by defenseman Noel Picard and sent flying through the air in what would become one of the most famous goal celebrations in hockey history. The sheer joy on Orr's face at having just scored the Stanley Cup–winning goal—and his complete disregard for the ice he's about to hit—has come to represent what the Stanley Cup means to those who play the game and to those who watch.

"I always tell Bobby he was up in the air for so long that I had time to shower and change before he hit the ice," said Glenn Hall about the most famous goal to get past him.

Orr finished off his record-breaking season with four trophies: the Hart Trophy as the league's most valuable player, the Art Ross Trophy as the league's top scorer, the Norris Trophy as the league's top defenseman and the Conn Smythe Trophy as the playoffs' most valuable player. The Bruins continued to dominate the early 1970s with their Stanley Cup–winning ways (though the Montréal Canadiens would be the champions in 1971) with another Cup victory in 1972.

Chapter Sixteen

The Team of Brotherly Love

When the NHL first expanded, adding six new teams, they kept the original six teams in the eastern division and put the new teams into the western division. The problem with this system was that the expansion clubs, being weaker teams, had no chance against the stronger original six during the regular season or in the playoffs. The St. Louis Blues were a perfect example of this talent discrepancy, leading the western division during the regular season and winning all their rounds in the playoffs. But each time they made it to the finals, they were swept all three times from 1968 to 1970 by an eastern division team.

Western coaches were well aware of this problem. "We're getting thrown to the lions," said St. Louis Blues coach Scotty Bowman. "I've known for a long time that we can't compete with the eastern teams with what we've got."

Even when the league mixed up the teams and sent the Chicago Blackhawks to the western division, the Blackhawks ended up on top of the division and made it all the way to the finals, eventually losing to the Montréal Canadiens. Things didn't start to change until the 1973–74 season, when the Philadelphia Flyers bashed their way to the top of the western division and were just one point behind the Boston Bruins for the President's Trophy (awarded to the team with the most points at the end of the regular season).

During the 1972–73 season, the Philadelphia Flyers finished with their first winning record since joining the league in 1967. Leading the way for the Flyers that season was a young Bobby Clarke, whose skill in front of the net earned him second place in the NHL scoring race (behind Phil Esposito) with 104 points. Rounding out the Flyers offense were big forwards such as Rick MacLeish, Reggie Leach and Bill Barber—all three players 50-goal scorers during their time in Philadelphia uniforms. The team would earn the nickname the "Broad Street Bullies" for the aggressive style of players such as Dave "the Hammer" Schultz, Don Saleski and Andre "Moose" Dupont. The Flyers might not have won all their games in the most convincing fashion, but the team always managed to get things done with a combination of offensive talent, excellent goaltending, sheer terror and the desire to win—a style dreamed up by the Flyers' astute coach, Freddy "the Fog" Shero, who counted on psychology being a big factor in hockey. If the other team knew you were going to hit them every time they touched the puck, then the next time one of their players had the puck on the end of his stick, he would think twice before deciding what to do, and that's all the Flyers required for motivation. Shero made sure his players knew his philosophy. "Get to the puck by the shortest route and arrive there in ill-humor," read the sign posted in the Philadelphia dressing room.

"We loved to go on the road and have people hate us," said forward Orest Kindrachuk in a *Toronto Sun* interview. "It made us play harder and fueled our desire. Our attitude was that it was our puck until someone came and took it."

The Flyers also had another weapon up their sleeves, and her name was Kate Smith. No, she didn't lace on a pair of skates, but it seemed that every time she sang "God Bless America" at Flyers home games, they won. Her record for the Flyers in the seven years when they occasionally substituted the national anthem for her "God Bless America" was an incredible 36–3–1. Whether it was the words to the song or the tone of her voice, something about Kate Smith's version of "God Bless America" inspired the Flyers, and they carried those winning ways into the 1974 Stanley Cup playoffs.

The Bruins easily won the league points race, with four of their players taking the top four positions as leading scorers. In the playoffs, the Bruins easily made their way to the Stanley Cup finals after defeating the Maple Leafs in four straight and the Blackhawks in six games.

The Flyers, meanwhile, had an easy time against the Atlanta Flames, finishing them off in four straight games. The story was a little different for the semifinal series against the New York Rangers. After losing the first two games, New York bounced back to tie the series at two games apiece. Both teams then traded equal 4–1 wins, sending the series into a decisive seventh game in Philadelphia. The Flyers were taking no chances. Before the game started, Kate Smith's "God Bless America" blared out over the speakers to the delight of the soldout crowd. With Lady Luck on their side, the Flyers jumped out to an early lead of 3–1 and never looked back, ending the game with a score of 4–3 and earning a trip to the finals to meet the regular season champions, the Boston Bruins. Kate Smith had done it again.

The Flyers' strategy against the Bruins would be the same as what they used against any other team—hit hard and play hard. Other teams made the mistake of treating the Bruins' top players, Bobby Orr and Phil Esposito, as invulnerable, but the Flyers played their own game, not giving the Bruins players any more respect than they reserved for other teams.

"Orr is not God," said Shero, getting straight to the point. "We've got to stop treating him like God. Let him take the puck, then hit him, make him work and hit him again."

Despite the well-thought-out game plan, Orr made the Flyers pay the moment they took their eyes off him. With less than 30 seconds left in the game and the score tied 2–2, the crowd at Boston Garden knew what was coming. As soon as Orr touched the puck and took two strides on the ice, the crowd rose to its feet in anticipation of a signature Bobby Orr rush, and they were not disappointed. Orr made his way through the neutral zone and between two Philadelphia defensemen, then slipped the puck past a surprised Bernie Parent for the game-winning goal.

Game two belonged to the Flyers, winning in Boston for the first time in their club's history in dramatic fashion after tying the game with under a minute left in the third period and then winning in overtime on a Bobby Clarke goal. Shero's system was working, but his team was only winning games by the skin of their teeth.

The Flyers tightened up their system, while the Bruins just seemed exhausted and unwilling to skate, losing game three 4–1 and game four 4–2. The Flyers were outskating the Bruins, and every line on the Philly bench contributed in the game. Boston limped back onto home ice to steal a game from the Flyers in a one-man show put on by Bobby Orr, who set up the first goal and then scored two goals of his own. But the night was remembered less for its offense than for the amount of blood that was spilled on the ice during the 60 minutes of play. The referees and linesmen were kept busy calling 43 penalties and having to break up six different fights as well as countless mixups in the corners and in front of the net. When the smoke cleared and the spearing, fighting, crosschecking and slashing penalties had been served, the Bruins took the game by a score of 5–1, and as the Flyers made their way off the ice, they heard the Boston fans singing in a sarcastic tone, "God Bless America."

In Philadelphia, the Flyers organization countered the Boston fans taunting use of "God Bless America" and called in Kate Smith to sing the song live before the game, hoping to inspire the team so that they wouldn't need to take the series into a seventh game in Boston. The song seemed to have the same effect on the Bruins, however, as they came out fast in the first period, peppering Parent with shot after shot. But no matter how hard they tried, Parent could not be beaten. The Bruins' momentum was taken away on a lucky goal by the Flyers' Rick Macleish, who deflected the puck off his leg, then off his skate and into the net while making a nuisance of himself in front of Bruins goaltender Gilles Gilbert. It wasn't pretty, but the Flyers were not a pretty team—a goal is a goal, and they had the lead. The Flyers held onto the lead through the second and third periods. The Bruins just couldn't get their offense skating, and when they did get off a weak shot, Parent made the easy save with no rebounds. Time ticked away in the third period, and the Flyers fans at the Spectrum knew that they had won the Cup. At the sound of the final buzzer, the Flyers piled off the bench and swarmed around goaltender Bernie Parent. The Philadelphia Flyers had become the first expansion club to win the Stanley Cup. Captain Bobby Clarke accepted the trophy on his team's behalf and paraded the Cup around the ice for the fans to see, all the time smiling his famous toothless grin.

"This club has more courage than any club I've ever coached," said a very proud coach Shero after the game. "A team like this comes along once in a lifetime."

The Philadelphia Flyers proved that they were not just a one-hit wonder by making it into the final round of the playoffs again the following year, only this time they faced off against the Buffalo Sabres for the championship. The Flyers played the same hard-hitting and aggressive forechecking game that had won them the Cup the previous year, and they were facing the same type of opponent in the Sabres as the Boston Bruins had been just a year ago. Where the Bruins relied on Orr and Esposito to score, the Sabres bread-and-butter line was the famous "French Connection" of Gilbert Perreault, René Robert and Rick Martin. The Flyers' physical play kept the Sabres top line out of games one and two, giving the Flyers a 2–0 series lead with a 4–1 victory in game one and a 2–1 win in game two.

Game three was one of the strangest in playoff history. Ever since hockey had changed from being an outdoor sport to an indoor one, weather never really factored into what happened on the ice. All that changed in game three in Buffalo on May 20, 1975, when a heat wave swept across New York State. Memorial Auditorium had no air-conditioning, and with some 20,000 excited fans adding their own heat, the temperature at rinkside rose to an incredible 87°F, making the ice surface soft and creating a thick layer of fog. During the course of the game, the referees stopped the play and asked the players to skate around the rink to disperse the fog. When that didn't work, maintenance crews had to be called out to wave large sheets to get rid of the troublesome fog. The fog posed another problem other than just obscuring visibility. As the ice melted, noxious chlorine fumes were released into the air, making the players a little dizzy and forcing them to take relatively short shifts on the ice. Because of the distraction, the game was a high-scoring affair.

Buffalo goaltender Gerry Desjardins could not find the puck through the fog and let in three goals on the first five shots. The Sabres rallied with goals of their own, tying the score up 4–4 late in the third period to send the game into overtime. The French Connection line ended the game when René Robert broke into the Flyers' zone and took a shot from a bad angle that beat a surprised Parent, slipping between his legs when he lost sight of the puck in the fog.

With the heat wave still gripping the city, the Sabres managed another win on home ice in game four by a score of 4–2 to tie the series. But that was all the Sabres could muster. Backed by the angelic voice of Kate Smith, the Flyers won game five and took home their second straight Stanley Cup with a 2–0 win in Buffalo. Philadelphia celebrated another championship that spring and found themselves a comfortable little spot in the history books for their effort.

Chapter Seventeen

Montréal Back on Top

Dynasties were nothing new in Montréal. The history of the Canadiens is filled with great players and memorable Stanley Cup victories, but it would be difficult to match the Montréal Canadiens of the late 1970s. Throughout the decade, the Canadiens were a top team in the league, winning the Cup in 1973, but they really blossomed in the 1975–76 season under the coaching genius of Scotty Bowman. As well, the team included a selection of players that reads like a list of Hall of Fame inductees: Guy Lafleur, Yvan Cournoyer, Bob Gainey, Jacques Lemaire, Larry Robinson and goaltender Ken Dryden, to name just a few.

Montréal had a very good team in the early 1970s, but they were outshone by the offensive performance of the Boston Bruins and the tough defensive style of the Philadelphia Flyers. The Bruins had faded in the previous few years, their fortunes mirroring the ups and downs of their often-injured superstar Bobby Orr, but the Flyers were a bigger threat to the Canadiens' success, using their size to intimidate their opponents on their way to two back-to-back Stanley Cups. Montréal decided to set the tone for the new season in an exhibition game between the two clubs held in Philadelphia. With the Canadiens up 6–2 in the late stages of the game, Philly captain Bobby Clarke ran into Canadien Doug Risebrough and started a fight that would clear both benches. The normally tough "Broad Street Bullies" were surprised by the Canadiens' sudden attack and were beaten up pretty badly in front of their home crowd.

"We won the Stanley Cup that night. It just wasn't official until next May," said Montréal left winger Steve Shutt following the Canadiens' playoff championship.

With all parts of the Canadiens' system playing at their best, the team finished out the regular season with a record of 58 wins, 11 losses and 11 ties for an NHL record 127 points. Montréal's first opponent at the start of the playoffs would be the Smythe Division winner, the Chicago Blackhawks. However, the Hawks provided little challenge for the Canadiens, who finished them off in convincing fashion in a four-game sweep, with Chicago only managing three goals on Dryden for the entire series. Montréal then met the New York Islanders and easily won that series in five games. Everything was working to their advantage because they had the other teams playing their style of game, and with players such as Bob Gainey, Doug Jarvis, Larry Robinson and Guy Lapointe imposing their defensive game, opposing teams had little room on the ice to make a play. The result was a virtually penalty-free, open game that was dominated completely by the Canadiens.

Many thought that the finals, which pitted the Canadiens against the defending champion Philadelphia Flyers, would be a bloodbath, but the Flyers had already learned their lesson earlier and tried to beat the Canadiens at their own game. Montréal took the first two games at the Montréal Forum, and not even the voice of Kate Smith could save the Flyers from a series sweep, as Montréal outplayed every team on their way to the top.

During the following season in 1976–77, the Canadiens were in a class of their own, posting the most successful record in National Hockey League history with 60 wins, 8 losses and 12 ties for a total of 132 points. On home ice, the Canadiens were almost perfect, with a 33–1–6 record.

Despite the amazing record, playing in Montréal was not (and to this day still isn't) an easy task for a player, with such a successful history to live up to and fans who demanded only the best from their team. It was the job of the coach to deflect, or even in some cases use, the media spotlight to his advantage, and Bowman was a master tactician. As with many great teams, the only true challenge they faced was from within. How many times has a team dominated in the regular season, only to lose in the playoffs to a "lesser" team? Bowman knew this could happen to his team, so he focused his players' energies on himself.

"We had such a good team that petty little grievances could develop that bring the team down. So what Scotty did, he made himself the focal point," said defenseman Larry Robinson. "The one thing that we had in common was that everybody hated Scotty."

The players may have hated him personally, but they respected him as a coach in every decision he made, and that's what mattered in the end. So when it came time for the Canadiens to defend their Stanley Cup championship in the 1977 playoffs, many sportswriters and fans saw a Montréal win as a foregone conclusion. The unlucky St. Louis Blues were the first team to play the Canadiens in the opening round of the playoffs. Although the Blues had finished first in the Smythe Division, they were no match for the Canadiens, who outscored them 19–4 in a four-game sweep.

The next round against the New York Islanders was a slightly different story. With players such as Mike Bossy, Denis Potvin and Bryan Trottier and the goaltending of Billy Smith, the Islanders gave the Canadiens a minor scare, winning games three and five. But they were still not the team that would become a dynasty in the 1980s, and they were taken out of the playoffs in game six after losing 2–1 in a tight defensive game. The Boston Bruins were next in line.

In their entire history in the National Hockey League, the Boston Bruins had never won a playoff series against the Montréal Canadiens, and the two teams had played each other an amazing 13 times. History would not change yet for the Bruins, and they lost the first two games by scores of 7–3 and 3–0, allowing the Canadiens to coast to their second straight Stanley Cup and a near sweep of the NHL trophies. Guy Lafleur took home the Hart, Art Ross, Pearson and Conn Smythe Trophies; Larry Robinson took home the Norris as top defenseman; Scotty Bowman took home the Adams Trophy as top coach; and the

Vezina Trophy went to the goaltending tandem of Ken Dryden and Michel Larocque for fewest goals against.

Over the next two years, the Montréal Canadiens dominated the National Hockey League with their talent-rich team, handing Boston another final-round defeat in 1978 and beating the New York Rangers in the 1979 Stanley Cup final. Things changed drastically for the Canadiens during the off-season after their fourth straight Stanley Cup win. Tired of the pressures of life in the NHL and Montréal, Ken Dryden announced his retirement to pursue other career options. Scotty Bowman did the same and switched allegiances to the Buffalo Sabres, hoping for a new challenge himself. The time in the spotlight for the Montréal Canadiens was over, and a new team from another island would take their place.

Chapter Eighteen

The New League Dynasty

When they first enter the NHL, most expansion teams spend their first few seasons at the bottom of their division, working out the kinks in their system before they can truly challenge the more established teams. Although they gradually improved throughout the 1970s, the New York Islanders still hadn't blossomed into the dynasty of the 1980s, but the addition of key players such as Mike Bossy, Bryan Trottier and Clark Gilles would assure the Isles a successful future. The team would come close to taking the Cup in the late 1970s, but they had to compete against the Philadelphia Flyers and the Montréal Canadiens at their peak. However, the Isles wouldn't have to wait long for their turn.

The Islanders finally got their chance in the 1980 playoffs. They finished with a respectable 91 points during the regular season but were not favored in the race for Lord Stanley's Cup. The Philadelphia Flyers and the defending-champion Montréal Canadiens were at the top of the league and had some of the better veteran players, but as everyone who knows something about hockey will say, the playoffs are a whole new season, and the 1980 playoffs would be all about the New York Islanders.

In the preliminary rounds, the Isles easily took out the Los Angeles Kings, and in an overtime-laden quarterfinals, they squeaked by the Boston Bruins in five games and the Buffalo Sabres in a high-scoring six-game series to make it to the Stanley Cup finals for the first time in the franchise's history. It wasn't going to be an easy win for the Islanders—they were facing a Philadelphia powerhouse that had finished the regular season on top of the NHL with 116 points.

The final series turned out to be one of the most exciting in recent memory after the long four years of domination by the Montréal Canadiens. The first game in Philadelphia was a close one, with the Islanders coming out on top 4–3 in overtime, but game two saw everything open up, and the Flyers delivered a very clear message with an 8–3 pounding. The Islanders regrouped and returned the favor with two straight wins, with all lines contributing to 6–2 and 5–2 victories to take a 3–1 series lead. Philly took game five easily by a score of 6–3 before a nervous home crowd to stay alive and send the series into game six.

Philadelphia coach Pat Quinn decided to tighten up on defense for game six in order to hold off the powerful offensive unit of the Islanders. He was hoping to get ahead early in the game and use a tight defensive style to hold the lead. At first everything seemed to be working in the Flyers' favor, but the Islanders had the same plan in mind, and when the final buzzer sounded the end of regulation time, the score was deadlocked at 3–3. In the first few minutes of overtime, both teams were a little skittish to try any daring moves on offense, but as it looked like the game might go on longer than they wanted, the forwards took some chances on rushes, with the defensemen joining in right behind. Both teams had their chances, but neither Isles goalie Billy Smith nor Philly goalie Pete Peeters wanted to be the one to let in a goal. At the lucky 7:11 mark of the period, the game finally ended.

The Islanders flew into the Flyers' zone with the puck and got it back to the point. Flyers goaltender Pete Peeters searched frantically for the puck through a mess of bodies in front of the net, but pesky Isles forward Bob Nystrom wasn't going to move from his prime piece of real estate. Nystrom took some abuse in front of the net, but finally got his shot with just enough of a deflection on his backhand to put it over Peeters and into the net for the Stanley Cup–winning goal.

"I really didn't think it was going to go in," said Nystrom after the game. "I never scored a goal on my backhand all year. I had to get it high, and sure enough, it went high."

"Until that moment, we were considered a team of losers and chokers," said Islanders coach Al Arbour with a huge smile across his face after the game. "If Nystrom doesn't score, who knows what happens to our team?"

The Islanders were just the second new team to win the Stanley Cup since the league had expanded in 1967, and they would continue the tradition into the next season at the expense of the surprise finalists, the Minnesota North Stars. The Islanders were even better the next season, using the same mix of offense and defense that had made the Montréal Canadiens so successful in the late 1970s. The Pittsburgh Penguins were the only team to challenge them in the 1982 playoffs, losing to the Isles in overtime of the final game of the division semifinals. After that, it was smooth sailing for the Islanders as they took care of the New York Rangers, Québec Nordiques and Vancouver Canucks for their third straight Stanley Cup. They did it again the next year, making it all the way to the finals, this time against the Edmonton Oilers and their young team of future Hall of Famers. The Oilers would lose to the Islanders, but they learned their lesson for the 1984 playoff finals, when both teams met again. This time it was the Oilers who came out on top and started a dynasty of their own.

Chapter Nineteen

The Edmonton Oilers Stanley Cup Dynasty

From the late 1970s through the entire 1980s, a period sometimes called the "era of the dynasties," NHL hockey was dominated by only a handful of teams. It started with the four-time champion Montréal Canadiens, then the New York Islanders took the title another four times in a row, and then the torch was passed on to the Edmonton Oilers.

The Edmonton Oilers joined the National Hockey League after the World Hockey Association folded in 1979. While the New York Islanders ran away with the Cup, the Oilers were building up experience in their young team that they would need to make it all the way to the finals of the playoffs. Such a young team needed to mature, with Wayne Gretzky, Mark Messier, Jari Kurri and Grant Fuhr all in their late teens and early twenties. It didn't take them long to develop into the new scoring machines of the

National Hockey League. Gretzky scored 51 goals in his first season and would almost double that total just two years later with 92 goals. Messier and Kurri soon followed suit, climbing their way to the top of the scoring sheet and taking the team farther in the playoffs.

The Oilers' first taste of the playoffs came in their opening season, when they met the Philadelphia Flyers in a best-of-five series. Although the Oilers were eliminated in three straight games, they took two of the games into overtime and made the Flyers work for every point. In the 1981 playoffs, the Oilers surprised the hockey world by defeating the Montréal Canadiens in the opening round in three straight games of a best-of-five series, but then lost in the quarter-finals to the Islanders, whose tight defense and veteran lineup were too much for the young team. It took the Edmonton team another season before they finally made it to the big show. For the 1983 playoffs, the Oilers finally had all of the pieces put together to make a serious challenge for the Stanley Cup. They easily disposed of the Winnipeg Jets in the division semifinals and massacred the Calgary Flames in the division finals with scores of 10–2 and 9–1, paving the way for their first-ever appearance in the Stanley Cup finals against the reigning-champion New York Islanders. Although

Edmonton had the all-star power of Gretzky, Messier and Kurri, the Islanders were still too strong for the young team and disposed of them in four straight games. But the Oilers learned a valuable lesson in their Stanley Cup loss, and they would take that feeling into the next season and into the 1984 playoffs.

It was Stanley Cup finals or bust for the Oilers in the 1983–84 season. They finished the regular season first in the NHL with 119 points and established a record-high number of goals scored with 446. Many felt that if the Oilers couldn't win or at least get to the Stanley Cup finals, then they didn't have what it took to be true champions and would just fizzle in the playoffs like the Chicago Blackhawks of the 1960s. Once again, Edmonton easily took out the Winnipeg Jets in the division semifinals but had a tough time against the Calgary Flames in the division finals. The Flames battled hard in every game and took the series all the way to game seven, only to lose 7–4. The Minnesota North Stars were next on the list, but they were easily swept out of the way as the Oilers' scoring machine moved into the finals in a rematch with the Islanders.

This time the Oilers were prepared for the veteran Islanders squad, who looked a little overwhelmed by Edmonton's speed and skill with the puck. The first game of the series was a defensive anomaly for the Oilers, who won the game by a score of 1–0, their only 1–0 game of the year. The Islanders came back in the second game on the strength of their veteran talent, winning the game 6–1, but that was all the offense the Isles could muster. In the next three games, the Islanders could get very little by Grant Fuhr. The Oilers outscored them 19–6 in the last three games to win their first Stanley Cup championship in front of a happy home crowd. Joy was evident on the faces of the young Oilers team as they were presented with the Stanley Cup, something that they had all dreamed about since they first put on skates.

As captain, Wayne Gretzky was the first to receive the Cup. Holding it like his life depended on it, he screamed out: "This is why we play the game."

The feelings from the Islanders players were a little mixed in their first Stanley Cup defeat in four years.

"This is the most disappointed I've ever felt in my life," said a distressed Mike Bossy, who had wanted to tie the 1960s Montréal Canadiens' five Cups in a row.

The feeling was a little less negative from teammate Denis Potvin: "When I leave this building, I am going to hold my head high."

The following year, Edmonton would finish off the regular season a few points behind the Philadelphia Flyers, but the playoffs would be even more successful for the defending champs. They beat the Los Angeles Kings, Winnipeg Jets and Chicago Blackhawks in convincing fashion on their way to the finals. The Oilers easily repeated as Cup champions, defeating the Philadelphia Flyers in five games thanks to Jari Kurri's record-tying 19 goals in the playoffs and set themselves up for a "three-peat" in the 1985–86 playoffs. Although the Oilers finished the regular season on a high note, with Gretzky breaking his own points record with 215 points and the team finishing atop the league, things would turn a little sour once the playoffs came around, and a team of rookies from Montréal would take the advantage.

Chapter Twenty

Luck of the Draw

The success of the Edmonton Oilers dynasty of the 1980s was interrupted by a fluke goal, and a rookie-filled Montréal Canadiens squad took advantage of the champions to become champions in their own right.

The 1985–86 incarnation of the Montréal Canadiens was a mediocre team that finished second in their division and seemed poised for an early exit once the playoffs started. Head coach Jean Perron knew he had a young team, but he was confident that with some good goaltending and a little luck, they could challenge for the Stanley Cup.

Edmonton, on the other hand, was confident going into the playoffs. They had managed to score 426 goals during the season and finished first overall despite the National Hockey League enforcing the "Edmonton Rule," which allowed player substitutions on coincidental minor penalties, thereby eliminating the four-on-four situations that favored teams with a high-powered offense like the Oilers.

The Canadiens started off the playoffs against long-time division rivals the Boston Bruins, and with rookie goaltender Patrick Roy making key saves during the best-of-five series, the Canadiens won three straight close games. The Canadiens division-finals surprise opponents were the Hartford Whalers, who had defeated the Québec Nordiques in convincing fashion in three straight games, winning the last one by a score of 9–4. The Canadiens-Whalers series was a hard-fought, back-and-forth bunch of games that could go to either team, and after the Whalers won game six 1–0, game seven promised to be a good one. The game was a close affair, with both Patrick Roy and Mike Liut making acrobatic saves to keep their respective teams in the game, and after three periods, the game went into overtime tied 1–1. The Canadiens dominated the first few minutes of overtime, and with just 5:55 gone in the period, rookie Claude Lemieux blasted the puck by Mike Liut for the series winner.

In the meantime, the Edmonton Oilers had finished off the Vancouver Canucks in three straight games in the division semifinals, outscoring them by a ridiculous 17–5. In the division finals, Edmonton was put up against their provincial rivals, the Calgary Flames, in one of the most exciting, fast-paced and heartbreaking series in recent NHL history.

This time, the Flames were ready for the Oilers after Edmonton had eliminated them from the playoffs on two previous occasions in the 1983 and 1984 playoffs. Gretzky and his team of high-scorers got a serious wakeup call in the first three games, losing the first game 4–1, and were lucky to come out of game two with a win in overtime. In game five, Calgary went up in the series 3–2 after a convincing 4–1 victory in which the Oilers' snipers looked tired after the Flames' tough checking all series. Edmonton bounced back in game six to ward off elimination with a 5–2 victory. But the best was yet to come in game seven.

Edmonton's Northlands Coliseum was buzzing with excitement an hour before the two teams set foot on the ice in what would become known as a classic "Battle of Alberta." The game was a fast-paced, hard-hitting affair punctuated by some fantastic saves from both goaltenders, who kept the game tied at 2 goals apiece going into the third period. The deadlock was finally broken early in the third. After the Flames dumped the puck into the Oilers' zone to change lines, rookie Edmonton defenseman Steve Smith took the puck behind the net to wait for his teammates to get set up for the offensive rush, while keeping the puck away from the Calgary player sent in on the forecheck. It all came crashing to an end when Smith tried to pass the puck from his position at the side of the net. Instead of getting the puck up-ice, he shot it directly off the back of goaltender Grant Fuhr's leg and into the net. Realizing what he had just done, Smith put his hands over his head and fell to the ice in disgust. Not a good birthday present for the 23-year-old rookie. The Oilers tried in vain to tie the game as the clock ran out, and Calgary came out the winner. After the game, the Oilers' dressing room was eerily quiet.

"I feel terrible," said Steve Smith, surrounded by a throng of journalists. "This is the worst day of my life."

Gretzky felt so bad that he contemplated retiring from hockey even though he was just 25 years old. "I don't see Wayne Gretzky playing for a lot longer," he said, using the third person to distance himself from the moment. "How much longer, I don't really know. When I was 20 years old, I couldn't wait until next year. Now my attitude is to take it one year at a time."

The Flames, on the other hand, used the excitement of the win over the Oilers to defeat the St. Louis Blues in another long, hard-fought game-seven victory to move on to the final round against the Montréal Canadiens, who had defeated the New York Rangers to earn their spot in the final.

The Flames brought their momentum from the Edmonton and St. Louis victories into game one against the Canadiens and came out with an easy 5–2 victory over the young Montréal team. Canadiens coach Jean Perron made a few adjustments to his game plan for the second matchup, and Patrick Roy was simply outstanding in goal as the Canadiens bounced back with a 3–2 victory in overtime off a Brian Skrudland goal just nine seconds into the period. After that, it was all Montréal Canadiens. They won the next three games to take the series and brought the Cup home to Montréal as champions of the league. Patrick Roy took home the Conn Smythe Trophy as the playoffs' most valuable player and set himself up for future successes with a Stanley Cup under his belt in his rookie year.

Chapter Twenty-One

The Return of the Oilers Dynasty

The Oilers didn't stay out of hunt for the Cup for long, coming back to win it in 1987 against the Philadelphia Flyers and again in 1988 after exacting revenge on the Calgary Flames in the division finals, beating them in four straight games. Then they went on to defeat the Boston Bruins in the finals to take their fourth Cup in five years.

The dynasty was halted again in 1989 because of an event that occurred during the summer of 1988, when the Edmonton Oilers underwent a change that reverberates through hockey to this day.

Five days after Gretzky married Janet Jones, he received a call and was told that Edmonton Oilers owner Peter Pocklington was trying to trade him to another team. On August 9, 1988, it was officially announced that Gretzky had been traded to the

Los Angeles Kings along with Mike Krushelnyski and Marty McSorley in return for Jimmy Carson, Martin Gelinas, $15 million in cash and first-round draft choices in 1989, 1991 and 1993. The hockey world was left with hundreds of questions about why one of the most successful franchises at the time would trade their best player when they had just come off a Stanley Cup victory in which he was named playoff MVP. But the heartbreaking loss for Edmonton and for Canadian hockey fans in general was welcomed as a much-needed boost of energy for the American market, which needed a superstar to sell the game to new fans.

Despite the loss of their leader and highest scorer, the Oilers still finished with a respectable 84 points, just behind Gretzky's Los Angeles Kings in their division. In a strange twist of fate, the Kings drew the Edmonton Oilers in the first round of the playoffs, pitting former teammates against each other in a battle to advance to the next round. It would be Gretzky's new team that would come out on top, eliminating the Oilers in the seventh game. But Gretzky wouldn't celebrate for long, as the Oilers' opponents in the next round, the Calgary Flames, defeated them in four games and went on to win the Stanley Cup.

The Edmonton Oilers' faithful didn't have to wait long before their beloved team brought them back into the playoffs with a realistic hope of winning the Cup for the fifth time. This time around, they were led by captain Mark Messier as they made their way through the playoffs past tough teams such as the Winnipeg Jets (a 4–3 series), Wayne Gretzky's Los Angeles Kings again (a 4–0 series) and the Chicago Blackhawks (a 4–2 series). Finally, they met the Boston Bruins for the Stanley Cup. Boston had the top team in the league during the regular season, but could only come up with one win in the finals as Edmonton marched to their fifth Cup, led by 16 playoff goals from Craig Simpson, the veteran skills of Glenn Anderson, Jari Kurri and Kevin Lowe, some rookie help from Adam Graves and Martin Gelinas, and the Conn Smythe Trophy–winning goaltending of Bill Ranford.

They had managed to pull off a surprise win, but the players that were the glue that held the Edmonton Oilers together in the playoffs were eventually traded off bit by bit. Smaller market teams could no longer survive with an all-star lineup such as the Oilers had and still function as a viable business. Edmonton has seen many young, talented players pass through their doors since those glory days, but the chemistry required to recreate the dynasty of the 1980s has continued to elude the franchise.

Chapter Twenty-Two

The Penguins Mini Dynasty

J ust one year before the 1990–91 season, the Pittsburgh Penguins went a pitiful 32–40–8 for a total of 72 points, not enough to make the playoffs. The Penguins made a miraculous comeback the next season, even without their captain and star player Mario Lemieux (who missed 54 games because of back surgery), climbing their way to the top of the Patrick Division on the backs of players such as Mark Recchi, Kevin Stevens, Paul Coffey and late-season arrivals Ron Francis and Ulf Samuelsson. Lemieux would return to finish the Penguins' regular season on a positive note as the team headed into the playoffs to face the New Jersey Devils in the first round.

The New Jersey Devils were still far from being the team that would come to dominate in the late 1990s, but they put up a good fight against the Pittsburgh Penguins, taking the series all the way to game seven before bowing out completely and losing the final game 4–0. The Penguins moved on to the division finals against the Washington Capitals and easily defeated them in four games straight after losing the first game. The Boston Bruins proved to be a more difficult challenge for the Penguins, who lost the first two games in Boston, falling behind in the series and staring elimination in the face for the first time in the playoffs. Lemieux rallied the troops for game three, and the Penguins used that momentum to win four straight over a surprised Boston squad to advance to the Stanley Cup finals for the first time in their history. Pittsburgh would face surprise-finalist Minnesota North Stars, who had finished the regular season with a mere 68 points. But with some hard work, a little luck and some timely goaltending, they made it to the finals for only the second time in the team's history. This matchup was also the first time since the 1934 finals, when the Detroit Red Wings faced the Chicago Blackhawks, that neither finalist had ever won the Cup.

Guided calmly throughout the series by head coach Bob Johnson, the Penguins were the definite favorites going into the finals. Although they lost games one and three, Tom Barrasso was solid in nets, giving the Penguins the confidence they needed going into game six with a 3–2 series lead. For game six, the Minnesota North Stars forgot to show up to the game, and the Penguins scored eight straight goals to win the Stanley Cup in the most lopsided final game in National Hockey League history. For the first time in his career, Mario Lemieux raised the Stanley Cup above his head and took home the Conn Smythe Trophy as the most valuable player in the playoffs.

"Good draft picks and some great trades enabled us to build a strong team, allowing me to live out my ultimate dream. Finally lifting that Cup is the best memory I have of the game," said Lemieux, looking back at his first Cup title. "Knowing that I'd worked so hard to get to that point brought out indescribable feelings."

While the Penguins celebrated their Stanley Cup victory with parades and backyard barbeques over the summer, head coach Bob Johnson was battling cancer. When the 1991–92 season started, the Penguins were hoping to be led by their coach through another winning season, but the optimistic Johnson finally succumbed to the disease in November. Scotty Bowman, who was the Penguins' Director of Player Development and Recruitment, took over coaching duties and led the defending champions into the postseason. They finished off the regular season with a respectable 87 points and two players at the top of the scoring ranks: Mario Lemieux with 131 points in 64 games and Kevin Stevens with 123 points in 80 games.

The Penguins first-round playoff opponents, the Washington Capitals, gave them a scare by taking a 3–1 series lead, scoring 6–2 in game two and 7–2 in game four. But Pittsburgh once again rallied around the performances of its key players and the clutch goaltending of Tom Barrasso to win the next three games and the series to move on to the division finals against the regular season champs, the New York Rangers. The Rangers were a solid team that year but were physically exhausted after hard seven-game battle with the New Jersey Devils, and Pittsburgh took the series in six games. Boston proved to be no challenge for the Penguins offense in the conference finals, and Chicago also fell under the impressive tally of goals put in by the Penguins snipers. Mario had his second Cup, and Pittsburgh celebrated again.

"I feel fortunate to have been part of two Stanley Cup–winning teams," said Lemieux, whose name in French means "the best."

Chapter Twenty-Three

The 24th Stanley Cup

With more teams joining the league and the competition for Lord Stanley's Cup becoming longer and more difficult, the time of the dynasty had long since passed. Teams now had to battle a larger pool of players, all with only one purpose in mind. The 1992–93 season was a time of major change in the National Hockey League, as it welcomed two new teams, the Tampa Bay Lightning and the Ottawa Senators, decommissioned the league president in favor of a commissioner and expanded the league season by four games to accommodate the new teams—all this highlighted by the celebration of the 100th anniversary of Lord Stanley's Cup.

The regular season ended with the champion Pittsburgh Penguins on top of the league with 119 points. But with three new teams in the NHL, other stronger clubs feasted on the new franchises, running up their point totals to where seven teams enjoyed 100-plus-point seasons. Going into the playoffs, it was expected that the Pittsburgh Penguins, Chicago Blackhawks, Detroit Red Wings, Boston Bruins and Québec Nordiques would all advance to the second round. But expectations are one thing and reality is another. The playoffs have the ability to wipe the slate clean for the teams that finish with mediocre records and give them a chance in what is commonly referred to as the "second season," when hard work, heart and a little luck can get any team into the finals. The first round of the playoffs were cruel to the "stronger" teams, and all but the Penguins were eliminated, leaving the Stanley Cup open to all the underdogs.

In the province of Québec, a classic battle between two archrivals renewed itself for one last time as the Canadiens and the Nordiques battled for the right to advance to the next round. The series got underway before a sea of blue and white at the Colisée in Québec City, and the teams had battled to a 2–2 tie by the end of the third period, much to the nervous delight of the Nordiques fans. Game one ended on a goal from Scott Young, giving the Nordiques the advantage in the series to the relief of the capacity crowd. For game two, the Nordiques completely dominated the Canadiens, making Patrick Roy look like a rookie as they pumped

4 goals past the flustered netminder. After the second loss, Canadiens coach Jacques Demers was asked by the media if he was going to replace Patrick in nets for game three, but the coach stood by his veteran goaltender, knowing that when the pressure was on, Roy would always perform.

The Canadiens came back in game three on the strength of Patrick Roy's return to form in goal and the start of a record playoff overtime win record, taking game three 2–1 in OT off a goal from Vincent Damphousse. The rest of the series belonged to the Canadiens as Patrick Roy shut down the Nordiques snipers, and the Canadiens rookies stepped up and scored the much-needed goals that would propel them into the next round of the Cup playoffs against the Buffalo Sabres.

Always with a flare for the dramatic during the playoffs, the Canadiens won game one against the Sabres in Montréal 4–3 in regulation time and then won the next three games by the exact same score, though all the games were won in overtime. This was the first time since the 1970 Detroit-Chicago series that a playoff series had ended with the same score in every game. Montréal's overtime magic continued into the Prince of Wales finals against the New York Islanders, with two more overtime wins to bring their streak to seven straight. On the strength of their overtime wins, the Canadiens took a 3–0 lead in the series and only faltered in game four, losing 4–1 before finishing off the tired Islanders with a 5–2 victory. This was the first time back in the finals for the Montréal Canadiens since they had lost to the Calgary Flames in 1989. They wouldn't know who they were going to play for a couple of days, while the Toronto Maple Leafs and the Los Angeles Kings battled in one of the most entertaining series of that year for any fan of playoff hockey.

Toronto's path to the Campbell Conference finals was not an easy one. They came out of the first round of playoffs against Detroit with an overtime win in game seven, and then had a long, hard-fought series against the St. Louis Blues. They won that series in a slightly more convincing fashion with a 6–0 victory in game seven, but they were about to face their toughest challenge of the 1993 playoffs—Wayne Gretzky and a hot Los Angeles squad.

All of Canada was excited at the possibility of a Stanley Cup final between Montréal and Toronto. The two bitter rivals had not faced off against each other since the 1967 finals, and it would have been the perfect story to cap off the

100th anniversary of the Stanley Cup. But one player had a different ending in mind.

Wayne Gretzky hadn't been to the Stanley Cup finals since he left the Edmonton Oilers and joined the Los Angeles Kings organization. Toronto looked like they had the series in hand with an overtime win in game five to give them the 3–2 advantage in the series, but Los Angeles bounced back with a controversial overtime win to stay alive and force a seventh game. The win was controversial because right before the goal, Gretzky had high-sticked Leafs forward Doug Gilmour, drawing blood. It should have been an automatic penalty, regardless whether it had been intentional or an accident, but the call was overlooked and Gretzky ended up scoring the winning goal. Like it or not, the Leafs were going to a seventh and deciding game. In what Gretzky himself calls his greatest game, he scored a hat trick and added an assist to lead the Kings to their first-ever Stanley Cup finals. This would be Montréal's 34th appearance in the finals.

In game one, the Kings looked like the team that wanted to win the Cup more, taking the match easily by a score of 4–1 on the back of Wayne Gretzky's goal and 3 assists. Montréal was determined not to hand the Cup over to the Kings, and Patrick Roy kept his young team in the game with some spectacular saves in game two. But that still wasn't enough, as the Kings had a 2–1 lead with the third period ticking away. Facing a 2–0 series deficit, Montréal head coach Jacques Demers made a controversial call that changed the course of the series.

Acting on a tip from one of his players, Demers made a risky call to have Marty McSorley's stick measured for an illegal curve. Demers nervously paced on the Canadiens bench while officials measured the stick. The stick turned out to have an illegal curve, and McSorley was penalized for the remainder of regulation time for the infraction. Montréal defenseman Eric Desjardins scored the equalizer to send the game into overtime. It took just 51 seconds of overtime for Desjardins to score his third goal of the game, giving the Canadiens the much-needed victory and, better still, the momentum in the series.

After the game, Los Angeles Kings head coach Barry Melrose was obviously upset by Demers' tactics. "I don't believe in winning that way."

Montréal, on the other hand, was flying high after their overtime win. "Without being cocky, when it comes to overtime, we just feel we can win," said head coach Jacques Demers after the Canadiens' game two overtime win made it their eighth straight victory.

The Canadiens managed another overtime victory on a goal by their big forward, John LeClair, in game three to take a 2–1 series lead. The Kings seemed to have lost all their energy after the heartbreaking overtime losses. The Canadiens kept Gretzky from stealing the show with a great checking game and relied heavily on the goaltending of Patrick Roy. The Montréal goalie's confidence was so high that in overtime of game four, after he robbed Kings forward Tomas Sandstrom of a sure goal, he goaded the player further by winking at him.

It was do-or-die time for the Los Angeles Kings in game five at the Montréal Forum. The Canadiens had not won the Cup on home ice since 1979, and on this night, the Forum was packed to capacity with an army of fans hoping to end the series at home. After the first period, it was obvious the Kings just didn't have what it took to mount a proper comeback, and they lost the final game by a score of 4–1. The Canadiens players launched their gloves in the air and swarmed around their star goaltender. Patrick Roy had proved once again that he was a clutch goaltender, and he took home the Conn Smythe Trophy for his efforts.

"I'm so proud of this team," said Demers after the win. "There were so many favorites, but we never stopped believing. We were like the boxer who didn't want to go down."

In the Los Angeles dressing room, things weren't as cheerful. "We're at a loss for words," said captain Wayne Gretzky.

It was the perfect ending to the National Hockey League's 75th anniversary and the Stanley Cup's 100th that the league's most storied and most decorated team took home the Cup that year.

Chapter Twenty-Four

The Curse is Ended

The last time the New York Rangers had tasted victory from the mouth of the Stanley Cup was in the spring of 1940, when the Broadway Blues defeated the Toronto Maple Leafs in six games. Back then, they were led by their top scorer, Bryan Hextall, and supported in nets by the outstanding goaltending of Dave Kerr. In the moments following their victory, something happened to the Stanley Cup that—for those who believe in the sanctity and holiness of the Cup and that a greater being oversees its well-being (don't laugh, some people are true believers)—would put a curse on the Rangers.

As players celebrated by taking turns drinking champagne from the bowl, Rangers president Colonel John Reed Kilpatrick decided it was the perfect time to commemorate the fully paid mortgage on Madison Square Garden by setting fire to the deed in the bowl of Lord

Stanley's Cup. In the eyes of the true believers of hockey's number one symbol, the Rangers had desecrated the trophy and cursed themselves and all the Rangers to come to a future without the Stanley Cup.

As the years passed, fortune did not smile down on Madison Square Garden. The Rangers spent most of the next few decades at or near the bottom of the league, making the finals only twice and losing on both occasions. Despite Hall of Fame players such as Andy Bathgate, Chuck Rayner, Rod Gilbert, Gump Worsley, Ed Giacomin and Phil Esposito, over the years the Rangers struggled to make the Stanley Cup finals. On the two occasions they did, they were taken out by the Cup's curse, losing once in a game-seven double overtime and the second time drawing the powerful 1979 Montréal Canadiens as opponents.

Things got worse for Rangers fans when the crosstown rival New York Islanders won four straight Stanley Cups in the early 1980s. But the Rangers faithful stood by their team, still hoping to break the curse of 1940. The story of the curse had become so prevalent that Islanders fans would taunt the Rangers every time the two teams played each other by chanting "1940" over and over again. But the Rangers would soon have the last laugh.

With Mark Messier at the reins and a host of other Edmonton Oilers alumni on the team, the Rangers slowly began to improve their winning record, finishing the 1991–92 season leading the league in points for the first time since 1941–42. But after their first-place finish, the curse reared its ugly head once again in the 1992–93 season. The Rangers finished in last place in the Patrick Division and missed out on the playoffs. Proving that the season had just been an anomaly, the Rangers returned to the top of the league at the end of the regular season in 1994 and entered the playoffs as one of the favorites to take the Cup from the defending champions, the Montréal Canadiens.

The Rangers silenced Islanders fans when they beat the crosstown team in four straight games in the opening round of the playoffs. They had an equally easy time with the Washington Capitals, who failed to mount any kind of offense and lost the series in five games. For the conference finals against the New Jersey Devils, the Rangers would not have such easy going, playing against one of the strongest defensive teams and one of the best young goaltenders in the game.

The Rangers had let the Devils take a 3–2 series lead through a simple lack of ability to score on the rookie Devils goaltender, who did everything but stand on his head to keep his team alive. Newspaper headlines across New York screamed that the curse was back once again to rob the Rangers of their best chance in years to take home the Cup.

"It wasn't like you could avoid it," said Nick Kypreos about the supposed curse. "It was everywhere—in the newspapers, on TV, from the fans."

But Rangers captain Mark Messier had a different ending in mind for his team. He told a few teammates in the dressing room that they were going to go out and win game six and then take the series in game seven. When his words got out into the press, they took on a life of their own and inspired the Rangers to greater heights.

Although the Devils came out with a 2–0 lead after the first period, Alexei Kovalev brought the Rangers within one in the second. Then it was Messier's turn to take control and deliver on his promise. Messier put in the tying goal with a beautiful backhand past Martin Brodeur off a Kovalev pass and scored the winning goal by punching in a Kovalev rebound. Messier further punctuated his message to his teammates when he scored his third goal of the game into an empty net. With momentum on their side, the Rangers took game seven and went on to the Stanley Cup finals for only the third time since they had last won the Cup.

The Vancouver Canucks had not been the best team during the regular season, but they played like a first-place team throughout the entire playoffs, backed by the solid goaltending of Kirk Maclean. But the Rangers were riding high after their inspired comeback win against the Devils, and they were not about to let the curse return to the Rangers' dressing room. Although Vancouver took game one in overtime, they lost the next three games, falling behind 3–1 in the series and facing elimination in game five back at Madison Square Garden. The Rangers began to prepare themselves for their first Stanley Cup celebration in 54 years when they took a 3–1 lead after the first period. Things suddenly turned bad for New York after the Stanley Cup was brought out from its storage place in preparation for the end of the game, and the Canucks magically scored 5 straight goals to win the game 6–3. When the Canucks won game six to send the series into the deciding seventh game, it looked like the curse was once again rearing its ugly head.

It was do-or-die time for the Rangers. Back in Madison Square Garden for game seven, the Rangers could not shake the feeling that the curse would once again ruin their chance at Stanley Cup glory. The Garden was packed with screaming fans hoping that their beloved team could pull off just one more win to break the 54-year Stanley Cup drought. There was tense excitement in the air late in the third period, with the Rangers up 3–2 on Vancouver. With the Cup waiting in the wings, no one in the building dared risk celebrating until the final buzzer had sounded. A hush fell over the Garden after a Vancouver player rang the puck off the post past goaltender Mike Richter, but that was as close as the Canucks would come. The final buzzer sounded the end of the game as well as the curse, and the Rangers piled off their bench and onto the ice for the long overdue celebration.

"For guys like Mike Richter, Brian Leetch and Messier, who truly carried the Cup burden, winning was unbelievable, like a 5000-pound weight had been lifted," said Kypreos.

For the fans of the Rangers who had stuck by them through all the bad years, it truly was an unbelievable moment.

Chapter Twenty-Five

The Return of the Red Wings

Not since the Detroit Red Wings beat the Montréal Canadiens in a thrilling seven-game series in 1955 had the Motor City's hockey team celebrated a Stanley Cup victory, despite making it to the finals six times up until 1996. While a curse had kept the New York Rangers from holding Lord Stanley's Cup, it seemed that the Red Wings simply didn't have any luck when it came to the playoffs. They always seemed to run into opponents who were at their peak, such as the Montréal Canadiens of the late 1950s and the Toronto Maple Leafs of the early 1960s.

It wasn't until the late 1980s and early 1990s that the Red Wings finally started to show signs of hope under the captaincy of Steve Yzerman and the coaching of Jacques Demers. At the end of the 1986 season, the Red Wings were at the very bottom of the National Hockey League standings with a pitiful 17–57–6 record. But just one season later under Jacques Demers, the Red Wings rebounded as a competitive team and made their first serious run to the Stanley Cup finals. That is, until they ran into the Edmonton Oilers and were easily dispensed of in five games. Lady Luck finally shone down on the Red Wings when the coach with the most wins in the history of the NHL joined the Detroit organization and turned a very good bunch of players into the best team in the league.

Scotty Bowman took over a team that included young players such as Sergei Fedorov, Keith Primeau and Martin Lapointe as well as grizzled veterans like Ray Sheppard, Steve Yzerman and Paul Coffey and quickly turned them into the premiere team in the league. In 1995, just his second year with the team, Bowman led the Wings into the Stanley Cup finals against the New Jersey Devils. With their combination of a high-powered offense and a veteran defense, the Red Wings were the favorites going into the finals, and the Devils had been written off by most sportswriters. But the neutral-zone trap employed by the Devils under coach Jacques Lemaire proved an effective weapon, and they ended up sweeping the Wings in four straight games.

The Red Wings returned more determined than ever for the 1995–96 regular season, finishing with the second-best performance in league history of 62 wins and 131 total points. But they still had the playoffs left to prove their worth. After easily polishing off the Winnipeg Jets in that team's last season before they became the Phoenix Coyotes, the Red Wings needed seven games plus overtime to defeat the St. Louis Blues to move on to the conference finals against the Colorado Avalanche. The series was a hard-fought battle between the two top teams in the league for the right to go to the Stanley Cup finals. But supported by the goaltending of Patrick Roy, the Avalanche would come out of the war the victors, beating Detroit in six games and eventually winning the Cup against the Florida Panthers in a four-game sweep.

The following regular season was not as successful for the Red Wings, as they finished in fifth spot overall. But it's in the playoffs where a team's winning record truly counts, and the Red Wings got off to a great start, defeating the St. Louis Blues in six games and then taking out the Anaheim Mighty Ducks in four straight. Then came the rematch against the Colorado Avalanche in the conference finals. The Red Wings were out for more than just a simple victory over the Avalanche—they wanted revenge. In the 1996 conference finals, Avalanche forward Claude Lemieux had delivered a vicious check from behind to Kris Draper, fracturing his nose and face. The worst part for many of the Detroit players was that Lemieux never apologized for the hit. Red Wing forward Darren McCarty never forgot the hit and sought his revenge the first chance he got. The moment Lemieux stepped out on the ice, McCarty grabbed him and began pounding him with his fists. Lemieux immediately fell to the ice and covered his face rather than take the punishment. Seeing his teammate in trouble, Patrick Roy skated out of his net to help his friend but was immediately tackled. Soon all the players on the ice were fighting— even both goaltenders got into the action. After all the equipment was picked up off the ice and the players had received their punishments, Detroit ended up winning the game and the series in six games, setting the stage for the Stanley Cup finals against the Philadelphia Flyers.

Although the Flyers were a strong team, they were no match for the Red Wings. Backed by the stellar performance of veteran goaltender Mike Vernon, they easily won the series in four straight games to take the Stanley Cup before their home crowd for the first time in 42 years. Detroit erupted into a week-long party.

But the celebrations were cut short when a limousine carrying Vladimir Konstantinov and

Slava Fetisov crashed into a tree. Fetisov emerged with minor cuts and bruises, but Konstantinov's career was over, and he was confined to a wheelchair for the rest of his life. Without Konstantinov on defense, critics had no trouble predicting that the Red Wings would not repeat as Cup champions. But led by their unflappable captain, Steve Yzerman, the Red Wings beat the Washington Capitals in four straight to take the Stanley Cup once more. As the Cup was passed around to each player, Konstantinov was wheeled out onto the ice for his moment with his former teammates. Detroit fans could now hold their heads high.

Chapter Twenty-Six

When Rules Go Wrong

For the start of the 1998–99 season, the NHL, in all its infinite wisdom, wanted to crack down on players interfering with goaltenders when they were in their protective circle near the net, and with that simple wish began a long, painful season of video-reviewed goals, angry coaches and blown games.

The rule, which already existed in some form but now was enforced to the letter of the law, stated that if any part of a player's body is inside the goaltender's crease when a goal is scored, the goal is automatically called back. This meant that if a player's toe so much as crossed the line, even if it did not interfere with the goaltender, the goal would be disallowed, most likely upon video review. The only players on the ice to benefit from this rule were the goalies, whose goals-against averages across the league were the lowest they had been in years, with only the four top goalies posting under 2.00 goals per game. Just two years earlier, not one goalie had broken the 2.00 mark.

Fans, owners and players all complained about the enforcement of the rule, but the National Hockey League, run by commissioner Gary Bettman, decided to see the decision through the playoffs. Throughout the history of the Stanley Cup playoffs, there have been many disputed goals, but none were more annoying and petty than those contested because of the in-the-crease rule.

It all exploded in the league's face during the Stanley Cup finals, when the Buffalo Sabres faced off against the Dallas Stars for league supremacy. Even though both teams had some talented offensive players, the series was noted for its defensive play and rather low-scoring games. But after five games, it was the Dallas Stars that had the advantage going into game six with a 3–2 series lead. Buffalo head coach Lindy Ruff was relying on his number one goaltender, Dominic Hasek, to force a game seven final with a win on home ice, but the Stars came out fast in game six and looked like the team that wanted to win more. But owing to some amazing saves by Hasek, the Sabres managed to stay in the game and force an overtime period with the score at 2 goals apiece.

Buffalo was fighting for their playoff survival as the Dallas Stars pressed hard into the Sabres' zone. The Stars piled several players in front of Hasek, hoping to sneak a shot by him. When the shot finally came in, Hasek managed to get a piece of the puck, but not all of it, and the puck fell just inside the crease area. Dallas forward Brett Hull swatted the puck in to win the game and the Stanley Cup for the Stars. The Sabres immediately protested to referee Terry Gregson, because Hull's skate was clearly in the crease at the time he put the puck into the net. However, Gregson made no effort to have the goal reviewed, probably because the Stars had already started their celebrations.

After the dust settled, the Sabres were still fuming over the controversial goal. "I'm very bitter because what happened," said Hasek. "It's a shame."

But no one was more upset than Buffalo head coach Lindy Ruff. "I wanted Bettman to answer the question why Hull's goal was not reviewed," said Ruff. "And really, he just turned his back on me like he knew this might be a tainted goal, and there was no answer for it."

That night, to the rest of the sports world, it looked like the league and the referees just didn't have the nerve to call back the goal after the Stars had started celebrating. But without the in-the-crease rule, the goal was a perfectly good one and normally would never have been questioned. Something had to be done to prevent the same situation from happening again. Two days after the Cup was handed to the Stars, the rule was officially changed to eliminate video reviews for crease violations. The decision did little to soothe the Sabres' fury, and the Stars will have to live with an asterisk beside their Cup win in the history books.

Chapter Twenty-Seven

Another Year With No Winner

In 1994, NHL hockey fans got their first taste of what it would be like to endure a winter with no hockey when the NHL Players' Association (NHLPA) and NHL management could not resolve a contract dispute and were forced to cut the season in half. Luckily for the fans, the two sides finally came to an agreement and continued the season at the halfway point, managing to get in 48 games before the start of the playoffs. Unfortunately, though, in their rush to save the 1994 season, the two sides left certain areas in the players' contract unresolved—a ticking time bomb that was likely to bring about the same results when the contract ran out 10 years later.

Fast forward 10 years to the 2004–05 season, and the contract dispute reared its ugly head once more. At stake was another season of NHL hockey and millions of dollars in lost revenue for the league, the players and the businesses that survive off professional hockey. The main issue of contention when it came down to it all was—money. Owners said they didn't have enough and wanted to put a cap on spending, including players' salaries. The players didn't believe that the league was in such a bad state as the league said, and thus began months of passing blame. There were some hopeful moments throughout the dispute, but by January it was clear that neither side would budge. For the first time in National Hockey League history, an entire season as well as the playoffs would be canceled. This was the only time this had happened since the influenza epidemic of 1919 had canceled the finals between the Montréal Canadiens and the Seattle Metropolitans.

For the first time, legions of fans were left for an entire winter with no hockey and were forced to reacquaint themselves with their loved ones on Saturday nights. Instead of watching the game, many people took out their skates and hit the local rinks, rediscovering the passion for the game that they'd had when they were kids.

After all the bickering and contract discussions, the NHLPA and league management finally came to an agreement on July 13, 2005, and hockey came back the following season. But the damage had been done. Some NHL players had retired, scoring records had been interrupted and most importantly, the Stanley Cup had not been awarded. Many people agreed with an initiative to have the Stanley Cup returned to its original purpose—to be given out to the best team in a challenge series. The league protested, saying that it had sole rights to the Cup, but finally capitulated before a court decision that if the NHL for some reason could not hand out the trophy to one of its teams, then the Cup would go to the team who best exhibited the skills and passion that Lord Stanley originally saw in the game of hockey. Only time will tell if this will ever come to pass.

Chapter Twenty-Eight

Stanley Cup Champions

Stanley Cup Winners

Year	Winner	W–L	Coach	Opponent
2005	Stanley Cup not awarded owing to labor disagreement lockout			
2004	Tampa Bay Lightning	4–3	John Tortorella	Calgary Flames
2003	New Jersey Devils	4–3	Pat Burns	Anaheim Mighty Ducks
2002	Detroit Red Wings	4–1	Scotty Bowman	Carolina Hurricanes
2001	Colorado Avalanche	4–3	Bob Hartley	New Jersey Devils
2000	New Jersey Devils	4–1	Larry Robinson	Dallas Stars
1999	Dallas Stars	4–2	Ken Hitchcock	Buffalo Sabres
1998	Detroit Red Wings	4–0	Scotty Bowman	Washington Capitals
1997	Detroit Red Wings	4–0	Scotty Bowman	Philadelphia Flyers
1996	Colorado Avalanche	4–0	Marc Crawford	Florida Panthers
1995	New Jersey Devils	4–0	Jacques Lemaire	Detroit Red Wings
1994	NY Rangers	4–3	Mike Keenan	Vancouver Canucks
1993	Montréal Canadiens	4–1	Jacques Demers	Los Angeles Kings
1992	Pittsburgh Penguins	4–0	Scotty Bowman	Chicago Blackhawks
1991	Pittsburgh Penguins	4–2	Bob Johnson	Minnesota North Stars
1990	Edmonton Oilers	4–1	John Muckler	Boston Bruins
1989	Calgary Flames	4–2	Terry Crisp	Montréal Canadiens

Year	Winner	W–L	Coach	Opponent
1988	Edmonton Oilers	4–0	Glen Sather	Boston Bruins
1987	Edmonton Oilers	4–3	Glen Sather	Philadelphia Flyers
1986	Montréal Canadiens	4–1	Jean Perron	Calgary Flames
1985	Edmonton Oilers	4–1	Glen Sather	Philadelphia Flyers
1984	Edmonton Oilers	4–1	Glen Sather	NY Islanders
1983	NY Islanders	4–0	Al Arbour	Edmonton Oilers
1982	NY Islanders	4–0	Al Arbour	Vancouver Canucks
1981	NY Islanders	4–1	Al Arbour	Minnesota North Stars
1980	NY Islanders	4–2	Al Arbour	Philadelphia Flyers
1979	Montréal Canadiens	4–1	Scotty Bowman	NY Rangers
1978	Montréal Canadiens	4–2	Scotty Bowman	Boston Bruins
1977	Montréal Canadiens	4–0	Scotty Bowman	Boston Bruins
1976	Montréal Canadiens	4–0	Scotty Bowman	Philadelphia Flyers
1975	Philadelphia Flyers	4–2	Fred Shero	Buffalo Sabres
1974	Philadelphia Flyers	4–2	Fred Shero	Boston Bruins
1973	Montréal Canadiens	4–2	Scotty Bowman	Chicago Blackhawks
1972	Boston Bruins	4–2	Tom Johnson	NY Rangers
1971	Montréal Canadiens	4–3	Al MacNeil	Chicago Blackhawks
1970	Boston Bruins	4–0	Harry Sinden	St. Louis Blues
1969	Montréal Canadiens	4–0	Claude Ruel	St. Louis Blues
1968	Montréal Canadiens	4–0	Toe Blake	St. Louis Blues
1967	Toronto Maple Leafs	4–2	Punch Imlach	Montréal Canadiens
1966	Montréal Canadiens	4–2	Toe Blake	Detroit Red Wings
1965	Montréal Canadiens	4–3	Toe Blake	Chicago Blackhawks
1964	Toronto Maple Leafs	4–3	Punch Imlach	Detroit Red Wings
1963	Toronto Maple Leafs	4–1	Punch Imlach	Detroit Red Wings
1962	Toronto Maple Leafs	4–2	Punch Imlach	Chicago Blackhawks
1961	Chicago Blackhawks	4–2	Rudy Pilous	Detroit Red Wings
1960	Montréal Canadiens	4–3	Toe Blake	Toronto Maple Leafs

Year	Winner	W–L	Coach	Opponent
1959	Montréal Canadiens	4–1	Toe Blake	Toronto Maple Leafs
1958	Montréal Canadiens	4–2	Toe Blake	Boston Bruins
1957	Montréal Canadiens	4–1	Toe Blake	Boston Bruins
1956	Montréal Canadiens	4–1	Toe Blake	Detroit Red Wings
1955	Detroit Red Wings	4–3	Jimmy Skiner	Montréal Canadiens
1954	Detroit Red Wings	4–3	Tommy Ivan	Montréal Canadiens
1953	Montréal Canadiens	4–1	Dick Irvin	Boston Bruins
1952	Detroit Red Wings	4–0	Tommy Ivan	Montréal Canadiens
1951	Toronto Maple Leafs	4–1	Joe Primeau	Montréal Canadiens
1950	Detroit Red Wings	4–3	Tommy Ivan	NY Rangers
1949	Toronto Maple Leafs	4–0	Hap Day	Detroit Red Wings
1948	Toronto Maple Leafs	4–0	Hap Day	Detroit Red Wings
1947	Toronto Maple Leafs	4–2	Hap Day	Montréal Canadiens
1946	Montréal Canadiens	4–1	Dick Irvin	Boston Bruins
1945	Toronto Maple Leafs	4–3	Hap Day	Detroit Red Wings
1944	Montréal Canadiens	4–0	Dick Irvin	Chicago Blackhawks
1943	Detroit Red Wings	4–0	Jack Adams	Boston Bruins
1942	Toronto Maple Leafs	4–3	Hap Day	Detroit Red Wings
1941	Boston Bruins	4–0	Cooney Weiland	Detroit Red Wings
1940	NY Rangers	4–2	Frank Boucher	Toronto Maple Leafs
1939	Boston Bruins	4–1	Art Ross	Toronto Maple Leafs
1938	Chicago Blackhawks	3–1	Bill Stewart	Toronto Maple Leafs
1937	Detroit Red Wings	3–2	Jack Adams	NY Rangers
1936	Detroit Red Wings	3–1	Jack Adams	Toronto Maple Leafs
1935	Montréal Maroons	3–0	Tommy Gorman	Toronto Maple Leafs
1934	Chicago Blackhawks	3–1	Tommy Gorman	Detroit Red Wings
1933	NY Rangers	3–1	Lester Patrick	Toronto Maple Leafs
1932	Toronto Maple Leafs	3–0	Dick Irvin	NY Rangers
1931	Montréal Canadiens	3–2	Cecil Hart	Chicago Blackhawks

Year	Winner	W–L	Coach	Opponent
1930	Montréal Canadiens	2–0	Cecil Hart	Boston Bruins
1929	Boston Bruins	2–0	Cy Denneny	NY Rangers
1928	NY Rangers	3–2	Lester Patrick	Montréal Maroons
1927	Ottawa Senators	2–0	Dave Gill	Boston Bruins
1926	Montréal Maroons	3–1	Eddie Gerard	Victoria Cougars
1925	Victoria Cougars	3–1	Lester Patrick	Montréal Canadiens
1924	Montréal Canadiens	2–0	Leo Dandurand	Calgary Tigers
		2–0		Vancouver Maroons
1923	Ottawa Senators	2–0	Pete Green	Edmonton Eskimos
		3–1		Vancouver Maroons
1922	Toronto St. Patricks	3–2	Eddie Powers	Vancouver Millionaires
1921	Ottawa Senators	3–2	Pete Green	Vancouver Millionaires
1920	Ottawa Senators	3–2	Pete Green	Seattle Metropolitans
1919	Series between Montréal and Seattle canceled owing to influenza epidemic			
1918	Toronto Arenas	3–2	Dick Carroll	Vancouver Millionaires

Stanley Cup Winners
Prior to Formation of NHL in 1917

Season	Champion	Coach (or *Captain)
1917	Seattle Metropolitans	Pete Muldoon
1916	Montréal Canadiens	George Kennedy
1915	Vancouver Millionaires	Frank Patrick
1914	Toronto Blueshirts	Scotty Davidson*
1913	Quebec Bulldogs	Joe Malone*
1912	Quebec Bulldogs	C. Nolan
1911	Ottawa Senators	Bruce Stuart*
1910	Montréal Wanderers	Pud Glass*
1909	Ottawa Senators	Bruce Stuart*
1908	Montréal Wanderers	Cecil Blachford
1907	Montréal Wanderers	Cecil Blachford
1907	Kenora Thistles	Tommy Phillips*
1906	Montréal Wanderers	Cecil Blachford*
1905	Ottawa Silver Seven	A.T. Smith
1904	Ottawa Silver Seven	A.T. Smith
1903	Ottawa Silver Seven	A.T. Smith
1902	Montréal AAA	C. McKerrow
1901	Winnipeg Victorias	D.H. Bain
1900	Montréal Shamrocks	H.J. Trihey*
1899	Montréal Shamrocks	H.J. Trihey*
1898	Montréal Victorias	F. Richardson
1897	Montréal Victorias	Mike Grant*
1896	Montréal Victorias	Mike Grant*
1896	Winnipeg Victorias	J.C.G. Armytage
1895	Montréal Victorias	Mike Grant*
1894	Montréal AAA	
1893	Montréal AAA	

Notes on Sources

Cox, Damien, and Gord Stellick. *'67: The Maple Leafs, Their Sensational Victory, and the End of an Empire*. Toronto: Wiley Press, 2004.

Devaney, John, and Burt Goldblatt. *The Stanley Cup*. Chicago: Rand McNally, 1975.

Diamond, Dan, ed. *Total NHL*. Toronto: Dan Diamond and Associates, 2005.

Dryden, Ken. *The Game*. Toronto: Wiley Press, 2005.

Dryden, Steve. *The Magic, the Legend, the Numbers: Total Gretzky*. Toronto: McClelland & Stewart, 1999.

Fischler, Stan. *Detroit Red Wings: Greatest Moments and Players*. Champaign: Sports Publishing, 2002.

Hornby, Lance. *Hockey's Greatest Moments*. Toronto: Key Porter Books, 2004.

Laberge, Stephane, and Sylvain Bouchard. *Les 100 Plus Grandes Hockeyeurs Québecois de la LNH*. Montréal: Éditions Hurtubise, 2004.

Leonetti, Mike. *Canadiens Legends*. Vancouver: Raincoast Books, 2003.

Liss, Howard. *Goal!: Hockey's Stanley Cup Playoffs*. New York: Delacorte Press, 1970.

McDonell, Chris. *For the Love of Hockey: Hockey Stars' Personal Stories*. Richmond Hill: Firefly Books, 2001.

McKinley, Michael. *Etched in Ice: A Tribute to Hockey's Defining Moments*. Toronto: Greystone Books, 1998.

Podnieks, Andrew. *The Great One: The Life and Times of Wayne Gretzky*. Toronto: Triumph Books, 1999.

Podnieks, Andrew. *Hockey's Greatest Teams*. Toronto: Penguin Studio, 2000.

Roxborough, Henry. *The Stanley Cup Story*. Toronto: Ryerson Press, 1964.

Turowetz, Allan, and Chrys Goyens. *Lions in Winter*. Scarborough: Prentice Hall, 1986.

Weir, Glenn, et al. *Ultimate Hockey*. Toronto: Stoddart Press, 1999.

J. Alexander Poulton

J. Alexander Poulton is a writer, photographer and genuine enthusiast of Canada's national pastime. A resident of Montréal all his life, he has developed a healthy passion for hockey ever since he saw his first Montréal Canadiens game. His favorite memory was meeting the legendary gentleman hockey player Jean Beliveau.

He earned his B.A. in English literature from McGill University and his graduate diploma in journalism from Concordia University. He has three other books to his credit: *Canadian Hockey Record Breakers*, *Greatest Moments in Canadian Hockey* and *Canadian Hockey Trivia*.